# The Ohio Free Will Baptist Pulpit
# 2016

Compiled by
**Dr. Alton Loveless**

This book was printed in the United States of America.

To order additional copies of this book contact:

**FWB Publications**
Enchanted Acres
1006 Rayme Drive
Columbus, Ohio 43207

FWB

# INTRODUCTION

Good preaching makes good reading
And Good reading develops good preaching.


Ohio has great preachers and their messages can help others as God inspires another for his preaching.


There is no substitute for God anointed study of His word and the thoughts of others to germinate in the minds of others.

May this series do this for you.

# CONTENTS

# 1

## How Many Ways Can You Kill?
### Dr. Tim Stout
### Heritage Free Will Baptist Church
### Columbus

**Revelation 21:8** *says "But the fearful, and unbelieving, and the abominable, and **murderers**, and whoremongers, and sorcerers, and idolaters, and all liars, shall have their part in the lake which burneth with fire and brimstone:...."*

**Murderers** - those who kill others or even hate others (**I John 3:15**).

This goes back to the question I asked earlier. Why is sin, sin? Answer: because it's a transgression against a Holy God! Our God demands holiness of us - without it we can't see God (**Hebrews 12:14b**).

God is so holy that the very thought of hate is murder (**Matthew 5**)! Not just the deed of physically killing, but the intent of hating someone is as bad as murder in God's eyes. We may not see that to the degree God does, but we are not as holy as God is! If we are not careful, we will allow our hatred for sin to become a hatred of the sinner. Never hate sinners! God loves them and we are to love them!

I want to remind us that in judgment, God will punish the sinner. Today He wants to be their Savior but someday He will be their Judge!

Several questions come up when we speak of taking the life of another. I feel I need to address something right here:

Sin has brought war! As long as there is sin, there will be war. We will have no peace until the Prince of Peace reigns.

Government is ordained of God - to have civilized behavior among citizens; we must have a civilized government. Therefore, understand **1 Peter 2:13-14** *Submit yourselves to every ordinance of man for the Lord's sake: whether it be to the king, as supreme;* **14***Or unto governors, as unto them that are sent by him for the punishment of evildoers, and for the praise of them that do well.*

**Genesis 9:6** says, *"Whoso sheddeth man's blood, by man shall his blood be shed: for in the image of God made he man."*

1. When we speak about taking someone's life, we deal with the subjects of murder and killing. Think about this - "All murder is killing but not all killing is murder." This is why war does not conflict with **Exodus 20:13** *"Thou shalt not kill."* Nations go to war, not individuals - God will judge nations / government (an institution He ordained). War is a consequence of sin!

2. Another example of this might be the police officer who is a Christian. He is an example of Christ and loves all people including criminals. He is not just protecting the innocent but trying to make a difference in the life of a criminal. There may come a time in the line of duty, a person you love, because of their offense may lose their life while your life is being protected. The lawman acts in his role to protect and do right.

3. Abortion is murder! Personally, I have a problem with any person who thinks this is okay when God says it's not! Just for the record, I will not vote for a politician who says he or she is in favor of abortion!

Abortion takes the life that began at conception. Here are the medical facts!

- Immediately upon fertilization, cellular development begins. Before implantation, sex of the new life can be determined.
- At implantation, the new life is composed of hundreds of cells and has developed a protective hormone to prevent the mother's body from rejecting it has a foreign tissue.
- At 17 days, the new life has developed its own blood cells; the placenta is a part of the new life and not of the mother.
- At 18 days, occasional pulsations of a muscle - the heart.
- At 19 days, the eyes begin to develop.

- At 20 days, the foundation of the entire nervous system has been laid.
- At 24 days, the heart has regular beats or pulsations (a legal sign of life).
- At 28 days, 40 pairs of muscles are developed along the trunk of the new life; arms and legs are forming.
- At 30 days, regular blood flow within the vascular system; the ears and nasal development have begun.
- At 40 days, the heart energy output is about 20% of an adult!
- At 42 days, skeleton complete and reflexes are present.
- At 43 days, electrical brain wave patterns can be recorded.  This is ample evidence that "thinking" is taking place in the brain.  The new life can be thought of as a thinking person at 43 days.
- At 49 days, we have the appearance of a miniature doll with complete fingers, toes and ears.
- At 56 days, we see a legal name change - from Embryo to Fetus.  All organs are functioning; stomach, liver, brain, kidney - all systems intact.  There are lines in the palms.  All future development of new life is simply that of refinement and increase in size until maturity at approximately age 23 years.  This is approximately two months before "quickening" yet there is a new life with all of its parts needing only nourishment.  I understand the mother doesn't feel the movement of the baby until about 4 months into pregnancy.

- 9th-10th week - baby can squint, swallow and retracts tongue.
- 11th-12th week - arms/legs move, baby sucks thumb, inhales/exhales amniotic fluid; nails appearing on fingers and toes.
- At 16 weeks / 4 months: genital organs clearly differentiated; baby grasps with hands, swims, kicks and turns somersaults (possibly not felt by mother).
- 18 weeks - vocal chords working.
- 20 weeks - hair appears on head; weight is about 1 pound and height about 12 inches.
- To take the life of a baby is the womb is murder!

4. What about Capital Punishment? Is it a sin to see a man face justice? Many "feel" that sin is a wrong thing but everyone sins so why punish it? [See **Genesis 9:6**; **Exodus 12:12**; **Leviticus 24:17-22**; **John 8**].

**Spurgeon** said "Sin according to these men, is a disorder rather than an offense, an error rather than a crime." Many see only a God of love, never a God of punishment. Over and over in Scripture you will find God is loving, gracious and merciful yet He punishes sin! That's why we die (**Romans 6:23**)!

**Ezekiel 18:20** says *The soul that sinneth, it shall die.*

Writing about Murder, John said (**1 John 3:14-15**)

*We know that we have passed from death unto life, because we love the brethren. He that loveth not his brother abideth in death.**15**Whosoever hateth his brother is a murderer: and ye know that no murderer hath eternal life abiding in him.*

# 2

## Homosexuality
(Romans 1:18-32)
Dr. Tim Stout
Heritage Free Will Baptist Church
Columbus

Let me begin my remarks here with two statements...God loves all sinners; no matter whom they are or what they have done.  This is not a sermon about our God of love hating anyone; it is about Him hating sin enough to give His Son as a supreme sacrifice! And yes, God loves all homosexuals! **Homosexuality** is a romantic attraction, sexual attraction or sexual activity between the same sex and gender.

Also, I have chosen to use Scripture and not current events.  We can begin with a strong Biblical statement that said God created male and female species of fowl and fish, cattle, beast and creeping things....and then He created man in His image.

Genesis 1:27 *So God created man in His own image; in the image of God He created him; male and female He created them.28 Then God blessed them, and God said to them, "Be fruitful and multiply; fill the earth and subdue it;...*

God created a man to be a man and a woman to be a woman! He created them to bring joy and fulfillment. And I like His plan! When God brought the woman to the man, Adam said WO-man!

J. Frank Norris stated about our verses in **Romans 1**, *"not only is <u>the righteousness of God</u> revealed, uncovered, made known, manifest, that everyone may see it. But the <u>wrath of God</u> is also revealed, uncovered, even as His righteousness."*

As we take a look at the sin of homosexuality, we might consider...
- The smoking plains of 5 cities mentioned in Genesis and see the ruins of Sodom and Gomorrah (**Genesis 19**).
- Because of sin, the city of Jerusalem was destroyed 7 times.
- Look at the effect of sin on Babylon, Tyre, Athens, Greece, Alexandria and Rome. In ruins! Why? Because the wrath of God was revealed and we are seeing daily proof of the wrath of God today!

**Romans chapter one** is a picture of 23 indictments against us with one result - death! Not just the physical death, but spiritual! We cannot deliver ourselves - we must trust Him. So why was God so harsh on this sin? Because it goes completely opposite of what He created man and woman to be! God calls it an abomination, not an accident. An abomination is something greatly disliked, abhorred and detestable.

As I deal with this I will use Scripture, not theory or opinion. I remember reading the words in **1 Kings 15:11-12** *And Asa did that which was right in the eyes of the LORD, as did David his father.* **12***And he <u>took away the sodomites out of the land</u>, and removed all the idols that his fathers had made.* The definition for "sodomy" is sinful sexual activity!

Some observations and then Scriptures:

I.  Decent, civilized people have always been against this monstrous perversion. I am not against the people - I am against their lifestyle. I have family and friends that have chosen this lifestyle and I do express my love and concern to them. There are consequences when one chooses to live like this! It is the same with abortion - God has ruled and we must adhere to His Word.

II.  Our permissive society lets crime go unpunished, so the sinful society becomes bolder. Some things that people "were" ashamed of are now boasted about. An example is how a young man or woman loses their virginity. It is made a glorified event instead of shameful prior to marriage.

III.  Television and Hollywood glorify the homosexual activity and sinful relationships. Our government seems to encourage "same sex marriage" with their legislation.

IV.    When society turns against God and the Bible, sin comes out stronger!

V.    God hates all sin and will punish the sinner for their sin. God loves all people - whether they are homosexual or heterosexual.

Now what does God say about homosexuality?

- They are called Sodomites and wicked sinners. **Genesis 13:13** *But the men of Sodom were wicked and sinners before the LORD exceedingly.* **Genesis 18:20** *And the LORD said,...their sin is very grievous;...*

- **Deuteronomy 29:23** says God overthrew these Sodomite cities *in His anger, and in His wrath.* Please keep in mind that God declared He changes not so we have reason to believe He feels the same way today about this gross and immoral sin!

- **Deuteronomy 32:29-33** *O that they were wise, that they understood this, that they would consider their latter end!* **30***How should one chase a thousand, and two put ten thousand to flight, except their Rock had sold them, and the LORD had shut them up?* **31***For their rock is not as our Rock, even our enemies themselves being judges.* **32***For <u>their vine is of the vine of Sodom, and of the fields of Gomorrah: their grapes are grapes of gall, their clusters are bitter:</u>* **33***Their wine is the poison of dragons, and the cruel venom of asps.* Their life is considered one of bitterness and unnatural abnormality and punishment is coming!

- **Isaiah 3:9** says *the show of their countenance doth witness against them; and they declare their <u>sin as Sodom, they hide it not</u>. **<u>Woe unto their soul</u>**! For they have rewarded evil unto themselves.*
- In Jeremiah, Lamentations, Amos and Ezekiel, God shows a likeness of whoredom and sodomy. **Deuteronomy 23:17 (see verse 18)** *There shall be no whore of the daughters of Israel, nor a sodomite of the sons of Israel.*
- When Judah sank to an all-time low in corruption, God saw that there were *"sodomites in the land: and they did according to all the abominations of the nations which the Lord cast out before the children of Israel"* (**I Kings 14:24**).
- When Asa became king, he did that which was right in the eyes of the Lord by taking away the sodomites out of the land (**I Kings 15:12**). King Jehoshaphat finished the work Asa began (**I Kings 22:46**). It is good to note that sin was dealt with by the king. The government realized the difference between sin and righteousness. Today what is called an abomination by God is accepted by man. How sad!

Some who are homosexual claim to be Christian. Where is the misunderstanding? Today just like the Bible days, Satan has sought to confuse immorality with the house of God (see **II Kings 23:1-8 (verse 7)**.

The Scripture is clear! A child can understand this - many just do not want to see it! Leviticus 18:22*You shall not lie with a male as with a woman. <u>It is an abomination</u>*

(something that is immoral, disgraceful, disgusting, or shameful). **(20:13)** *If a man lies with a male as he lies with a woman, both of them have committed an abomination. They shall surely be put to death.*

I will get into the passage in **Romans 1:26-31** in this series. As I do, I want to say something very important. Homosexuals are invited to attend this church. We love all souls and all sinners. I will preach what the Scriptures say and beg the Holy Spirit of God to speak to the heart of all of us! We have had those of this perverse lifestyle attend our services and come to know Christ as Savior, turning from that sin to a Savior that loves them. I bless the Lord!

The Lord loves to forgive. Christ came to show us mercy and pardon and offer us grace and redemption.

**Nehemiah 9:17** says *"...but thou art a God ready to pardon, gracious and merciful, slow to anger, and of great kindness, ...."*

**Proverbs 28:13** *He that covereth his sins shall not prosper: but whoso confesseth and forsaketh them shall have mercy.*

**Psalms 103:10-12** *He hath not dealt with us after our sins; nor rewarded us according to our iniquities. 11 For as the heaven is high above the earth, so great is his mercy toward them that fear him. 12 As far as the east is from the west, so far hath he removed our transgressions from us.*

Just a reminder here and then a question. God forgives sin - there is nothing else you can do to get to Heaven except trust Him! You are not perfect therefore you cannot trust your goodness and personal righteousness.

Guilt comes from the Holy Spirit as He points us to repentance and reconciliation. But, we do not have to live in shame and regret over our past choices - when God forgives us, we should forgive ourselves too.

**Sin! Do you overcome it or does it overtake you?** I confess my concern: if we are willing to commit sin in public, I am curious what we are doing, thinking, watching, and saying behind closed doors!

A.W. Tozer said *"We cannot grasp the true meaning of the divine holiness by thinking of someone or something very pure and then raising the concept to the highest degree we are capable of. God's holiness is not simply the best we know infinitely bettered. We know nothing like the divine holiness. It stands apart, unique, unapproachable, incomprehensible and unattainable. The natural man is blind to it. He may fear God's power and admire His wisdom, but His holiness he cannot even imagine." - The Knowledge of the Holy, 111.*

Remember, all of us have sinned (**Romans 3:10, 23**), therefore we cannot sit in judgment of others - the ***Word*** will be the judge!

**Thomas Kempis** said *"How rarely we weigh our neighbor in the same balance in which we weigh ourselves."*

**Revelation 22:14-15** *Blessed are they that do His commandments, that they may have right to the tree of life, and may enter in through the gates into the city. 15For without are dogs, and sorcerers, and whoremongers, and murderers, and idolaters, and whosoever loveth and maketh a lie.*

The whole race of mankind, in consequence of the fall, is infected with a most dreadful, fearful, soul-killing disease! You and I are infected with sin!

It's in our nature, and its effects are manifested in our conduct! Its seat is in the heart — which has become deceitful above all things, and desperately wicked!

**James Smith**, (New Park Street Chapel, London), in 1849 said...
- This *malignant* disease has spread over every faculty of the soul!
- The *understanding* is darkened — so that you cannot see your dreadful state!
- The *conscience* is defiled — and neglects its vital office!
- The *will* is powerfully biased to evil — and chooses what God abhors!
- The *affections* are earth-bound — and set on forbidden things!

- The *imagination* is become sensual — and only employed in evil!
- The *reason* is debased — and calls darkness, light; and light, darkness!
- The *memory* is captivated, and become a storehouse of iniquity!
- The *whole soul* is paralyzed, polluted, and diseased!
- Righteousness, before the fall, once lodged in it — but now murderers reside there!
- Satan has got possession — and endeavors to lead you to hell in a false peace!

# 3

## Drunkards
Dr. Tim Stout
Heritage Free Will Baptist Church
Columbus

**Drunkards** - those given to and overcome by alcohol.

Before dealing with "liquor" itself, I want to address the topic of "addictions." Today people are addicted to:
- Drugs and alcohol.
- Food.
- Sexual pleasure.
- Electronic devices.
- Work.
- Relationships - a destructive dependence on people.
- Gambling.

Alcohol and drugs create physical, emotional, and social dependence on artificially induced feelings. Some stimulants, ranging from cocaine to nicotine, produce an exhilaration that creates an illusion of well-being, power, adequacy, and control. Others cause hallucinations of pleasure or terror. If you have ever seen someone go through the DT's, you will understand what I am talking about.

Here is where part of the problem comes - Depressants, such as alcohol, can temporarily relieve our anxieties and our inhibitions and therefore many argue that it is a good thing.

Let me give some stats that ought to open our eyes to this:

- Percent of adults 18 years of age and over who are current regular drinkers (at least 12 drinks in the past year): 51.5%
- Percent of adults 18 years of age and over who are current infrequent drinkers (1-11 drinks in the past year): 13.6%
- Number of alcoholic liver disease deaths in 2011: 15,990
- Number of alcohol-induced deaths, excluding accidents and homicides in 2011: 25,692.

The harmful use of alcohol is a leading risk factor for premature death and disability in the world.

Worldwide alcohol causes 1.8 million deaths (3.2% of total) and 58.3 million (4% of total) of Disability-Adjusted Life Year. Unintentional injuries alone account for about one third of the 1.8 million deaths, while neuro-psychiatric conditions account for close to 40% of the 58.3 million Disability-Adjusted Life Year.

Alcohol is the drug of choice among youth. Many young people are experiencing the consequences of drinking too much, at too early an age. As a result, underage drinking is a leading public health problem in this country.

Each year, approximately 5,000 young people under the age of 21 die as a result of underage drinking; this includes about 1,900 deaths from motor vehicle crashes, 1,600 as a result of homicides, 300 from suicide, as well as hundreds from other injuries such as falls, burns, and drowning.

- Every day in the United States, more than 4,750 kids under age 16 have their first full drink of alcohol.
- More youth in the United States drink alcohol than smoke tobacco or marijuana, making it the drug most used by American young people.
- The average age at which young people ages 12 to 17 begin to drink is 13 years old.
- The average age that underage drinkers ages 12 to 20 begin to drink is 16.1 years old.

For years, preachers took a strait and sure stand against liquor. I've stood up against it in 2 communities where I have lived on liquor issues - stood against "liquor by the drink."

Pastors and evangelists used to preach about liquor in their meetings.

- Billy Sunday had a famous "Booze Sermon."
- Maze Jackson preached a message titled, "Following the Bottle"
- B. R. Lakin preached message, "Liquor, Beer, Wine, and Booze."

I am 53 years old and I have never heard a sermon in a revival on the woes of alcohol!  Where is the backbone of our preachers?  Then, I thought, I have mentioned it, but never preached a sermon on it.

Our Free Will Baptist Church Covenant says:

*"Having given ourselves to God, by faith in Christ, and adopted the Word of God as our rule of faith and practice, we now give ourselves to one another by the will of God in this solemn **covenant.***

*We promise, by His grace, to love and obey Him in all things, to avoid all appearance of evil, to abstain from all sinful amusements and unholy conformity to the world, from all sanction of the use and sale of intoxicating beverages, and to "provide things honest in the sight of all men."*

For the sake of preaching, I want to be sure we use Bible references.

### Proverbs 20:1

Wine deceives and mocks those who use it! It has been used to benefit in moderation, but it easily deceives people, therefore, we are "teetotalers."

## The Drunkards Progress

**From the first glass to the grave.**
 Step 1. A glass with a friend.
 Step 2. A glass to keep the cold out.
 Step 3. A glass too much.
 Step 4. Drunk and riotous.
 Step 5.The summit attained. Jolly companions.
       A confirmed drunkard.
 Step 6. Poverty and disease.
 Step 7. Forsaken by Friends.
 Step 8. Desperation and crime.
 Step 9. Death by suicide.

**Proverbs 23:20-21**. We are forbidden, not only to be drunkards or gluttons, but to be found in the company of such persons.

By the way, I do not believe Christ made nor drank "fermented wine." I have studied the laws of fermentation and also refuse to believe that Christ would do something and tell us it is sin! He never sinned!

A member of Alcoholics Anonymous once sent columnist Ann Landers the following:
- We drank for happiness and became unhappy.
- We drank for joy and became miserable.
- We drank for sociability and became argumentative.
- We drank for sophistication and became obnoxious.
- We drank for friendship and made enemies.
- We drank for sleep and awakened without rest.

- We drank for strength and felt weak.
- We drank "medicinally" and acquired health problems.
- We drank for relaxation and got the shakes.
- We drank for bravery and became afraid.
- We drank for confidence and became doubtful.
- We drank to make conversation easier and slurred our speech.
- We drank to feel heavenly and ended up feeling like hell.
- We drank to forget and were forever haunted.
- We drank for freedom and became slaves.
- We drank to erase problems and saw them multiply.
- We drank to cope with life and invited death.

There is not a person under the sound of my voice who is not guilty of this type of sin! We are all unclean, ungodly and unrighteous. No matter how good you may think yourself to be, our mouths are stopped before the Lord (**Romans 3:19**).

**But there is hope for all of us today!**

**1 Corinthians 6:9-11** *Know ye not that the unrighteous shall not inherit the kingdom of God? Be not deceived: neither fornicators, nor idolaters, nor adulterers, nor effeminate, nor abusers of themselves with mankind, 10Nor thieves, nor covetous, nor drunkards, nor revilers, nor extortioners, shall inherit the kingdom of God.*

**11***And such were some of you: but ye are washed, but ye are sanctified, but ye are justified in the name of the Lord Jesus, and by the Spirit of our God.*

**1 John 1:6-10** *If we say that we have fellowship with him, and walk in darkness, we lie, and do not the truth: ***7****But if we walk in the light, as he is in the light, we have fellowship one with another, and the blood of Jesus Christ his Son cleanseth us from all sin. ***8****If we say that we have no sin, we deceive ourselves, and the truth is not in us. ***9****If we confess our sins, he is faithful and just to forgive us our sins, and to cleanse us from all unrighteousness. ***10****If we say that we have not sinned, we make him a liar, and his word is not in us.*

The Lord loves to forgive.  Christ came to show us mercy and pardon and offer us grace and redemption. Because we cannot completely grasp His holiness, we have a difficult time trying to understand His love for sinners and His hatred for sin!

**Nehemiah 9:17** says *"...but thou art a God ready to pardon, gracious and merciful, slow to anger, and of great kindness, ...."*

**Proverbs 28:13** *He that covereth his sins shall not prosper: but whoso confesseth and forsaketh them shall have mercy.*

God forgives sin - there is nothing else you can do to get to Heaven except trust Him! You are not perfect therefore you cannot trust your goodness and personal righteousness.

# 4

## FOLLOWING THE EXAMPLE OF CHRIST
John 13:1-17
National Association
July 21, 2015
Dr. Danny Baer
Southeastern Free Will Baptist College
Formally from Ohio

I loved Roy Thomas!

I loved his preaching, I loved his stories, I loved his family. I had the privilege of working with his wife, Pat and his two children, Patsy and Mark.

I loved his passion for missions. Remember that map he used to take around the country. Brother Roy had a map of the United States and he had put a red dot on it for each Free Will Baptist Church in the country. He would point to those states where there were little or no dots and challenge us to reach the unreached. What a great ambassador he was for the cause of Christ!

I must admit, though, that when I looked at his map my eyes were also drawn to those areas that were solid red. Those were the portions of the country were there were so many Free Will Baptist Churches that it was impossible to distinguish the individual dots. In those areas he just colored in large sections.

There were a number of those areas, but one of the biggest ones was through the Appalachian Mountains and on either side in the foothills of the Appalachians. I grew up in one of those solid red areas in Southern Ohio.

I could walk out my front door when I was a teenager and look North, to the right of my home, and see the Union Free Will Baptist Church about a quarter of a mile away. That is where I had the privilege to serve as the youth pastor for Calvin Evans for a while. Go about three miles beyond Union and you come to my home church, Bloom FWB. Just beyond Bloom is the Frederick FWB Church.

Go back to my home and head south and in two miles you will see the Porter Free Will Baptist where Forest – Tarry Chamberlain pastored for so many years and Mark Price does now. Not far past Porter you come to the top of a hill and turn left to come to the Sciotodale FWB Church.
If you gave me 10 minutes, I could probably be to one of about 15 FWB churches from my home. Give me a half hour and that number jumps to about 40!

I lived in Free Will Baptist country. In fact, I thought Free Will Baptists were like that all over. I soon found out differently – especially when I pastored in Williamsburg,

Virginia where I got some mighty strange looks when people would ask me "What is a Free Will Baptist, anyway?"

Not only did I grow up in a Free Will Baptist church. I grew up in a Feet Washing Free Will Baptist church. Feet Washing was just as much a part of our church as Sunrise Service or singing out of the Church Hymnal. I thought all Christians practiced Feet Washing!

Now, if you thought I got funny looks in Williamsburg when I told folks I was from a Free Will Baptist Church, you should have seen the looks when I got to the Feet Washing part! I found out that the practice was rare among evangelical churches. In fact, I met some people who I consider great Christians who do not practice Feet Washing in their church – one of those being my own father-in-law whom I hold in high regard as to his faith in Christ and his Christian testimony.

As a young Christian, and later, a young preacher, I felt I needed to be sure of what I believed. I am not a skeptic, but I have examined very closely what we believe. I wanted to make sure that my faith is firmly founded in the Scriptures and not just in what I was taught in my home church.

So, I began a journey – one which I would like to take you through this morning, if you will allow me. I want to take us through three steps:
- The Basis for Feet Washing
- The Ordinance of Feet Washing
- The Practice of Feet Washing.

I.    **THE BIBLICAL HISTORICAL BASIS**
To understand any doctrine we must first go to Scripture. And, when we study the Biblical passages that apply we must also understand the historical and cultural setting. When this is done I believe that we can see about 4, maybe 5 levels to the basis of feet washing.

### 1. The first level is <u>Cleansing</u>

It is difficult for us to grasp the context of feet washing in our day and time.

As we all know, during Bible days most people traveled by walking on dirt or sand or mud roadways. The necessity of cleaning your feet was part of the mindset of the day. It would be one of the last things on our mind. We might kick off our shoes or wash our hands, but not our feet.

However, it was one of foremost things on the mind of people in those days as a matter of hygiene. And is implicit in many of the passages in Scripture.

Now, I submit to you, however, that this is not the purpose here in this passage. Jesus was not simply trying to get their feet clean. They had already had supper. The washing of feet would have taken place much earlier in the evening. Peter brings this up, but I believe that it is an attempt to sidetrack Jesus. But Jesus reprimands Peter, uses Peter's statement to give a quick lesson and quickly gets back on point.

## 2. The next level is <u>Hospitality</u>

This is where we find many of the references in Scripture.

When the three men/angels/theophany came to Abraham in Genesis 18 He said, "Let a little water, I pray you, be fetched, and wash your feet, and rest yourselves under the tree." He was being hospitable.

In the next chapter, Lot meets two men/angels and says, "Behold now, my lords, turn in, I pray you, into your servant's house, and tarry all night, and wash your feet."

You can find similar situations in the stories of Laban, Joseph and others.

It was not only part of the mindset of the people of that day to be compelled to wash their feet when they arrive at their destination, but it was embedded in the culture that you should offer water for a guest to wash their feet when they came to your house – just like I might say to you, if you came to my home for a meal, "the bathroom is just down the hallway on the right if you need to wash up before we eat."

Again, this was not the primary purpose in John 13.

## 3.    The next level is <u>Servanthood</u>

Historical scholars tell us that at times a servant would be compelled to wash the feet of a visitor or their master. There is not direct indication of this happening in scripture

– where a servant is involved—but the underlying assumption is clearly there.

In I Samuel 25, when the men of David went to fetch Abagail as a wife for David, she greeted them and said, "Behold, *[let] thine handmaid [be] a servant to wash the feet of the servants of my lord.*"

This concept of servanthood is definitely at play in this passage. In fact, it is the center of the point that Jesus is making when he set about to explain to his disciples what he had done.

Notice in verse 12. Jesus said, "*Know ye what I have done to you?*"

Have you figured out what's going on here guys? Do you get it?

"*Ye call me Master and Lord: and ye say well; for [so] I am. If I then, [your] Lord and Master, have washed your feet; ye also ought to wash one another's feet.*"

Jesus is saying, "If I as Master, have stooped to the level of servant to wash your feet. You, as servants, certainly be willing to wash each other's feet."

This hits home!!!

One huge problem with our society is the feeling of superiority.

I am better than others in this world!
I am better than others in my country!
I am better than others in my family!
I am better than others in my church!!!!
Jesus is pointing out that HE IS THE MASTER!!!
WE ARE ALL BUT SERVANTS!!!!!

*Dr. Picirilli*

*The basin and the towel we take*
*As emblems of our self-disdain*
*We gladly our own good forsake,*
*And seek, henceforth, our brother's gain.*

But there is yet another level.

## 4. Voluntary servitude or <u>Humility</u>

Not "forced" service -- but willing, humble service.

That was the spirit of Abagail, wasn't it?

That was the spirit of the women of Luke 7 and Mary in John 11 who washed Jesus' feet.

That's the spirit of Christ here.

He is the master! But, he is willing to take to form of a servant.

Dr. Matt Pinson in his book, *"The Washing of the Saints Feet"* ties this very quality with the incarnation. He makes a great point. Philippians 2:7 says that Christ, "made himself of no reputation, and took upon him the form of a servant."

This is the essence of the command, "ye also ought to wash one another's feet."

*Mary Ruth Wisehart*
*Emblems of thy condescension*
*Willingly we take up now*
*And with servant cloth and basin*
*Low before our brethren bow;*

However, I firmly believe we need to go one step further.

## 5. Voluntary, humble service motivated by love!

If you obey a commandment motivated by fear of harm or death--You are a forced servant – a slave

If you obey motivated by personal gain

-You are in indentured servant or an employee (hireling)

If you are motivation by love

-You are a willing servant – a bond slave – Christ like!

Even though love is not mentioned in this passage, there is no doubt Christ loved these men – and he wanted them to love each other.

In fact, just a short time later in verse 34 of this very chapter, Christ says, "A new commandment I give unto you, That ye love one another; as I have loved you, that ye also love one another."

Jesus wants us to love each other – and that's not just the "lovey" people, by the way.

Yes, he washed the feet of his beloved disciple, John, the one who would be at the cross the next day and take into his care the mother of Jesus.

But he also washed the feet of 9 men who would forsake him at his crucifixion.

He also washed the feet of the one who would deny him.

And, He also washed the feet of the one who would betray him!!!

**Jesus was wanting these men to willingly serve each other out of a heart of love. That is the lesson here.**

Jesus wants US to love each other as He has loved us.
        To willingly serve others.
                Even those who are hard to love!!!!

This is the Biblical basis for feet washing. This leads me to my second point – the ordinance.

## II.   THE ORDINANCE OF WASHING THE SAINTS FEET.

When you read or talk about ordinances two question seem to arise.

***The first of these questions is "how many ordinances are there?"***

Some might feel that there are more than three. Again, I would defer you to Dr. Pinson's book. He covers that concern well.

And some would limit the number to two!

In preparation for this sermon, I sent out an email inviting Free Will Baptist pastors to participate in a survey regarding Feet washing. Many of you here today received that and responded. And I thank you. Brother Van Powell, of South Carolina won the new Randall House Commentary on Matthew written by my good friend, Dr. Jeff Crabtree.

I obtained the email list and proper permission from our Executive Office. They had emails for just over 760 pastors.

Of those 760 pastors there were 366 who responded – that's a great response rate.

If you consider the total population of FWB pastors to be about 2200, having 360 respond gives my survey a margin of error of under 5 percent.

By the way, I have prepared a document which shows the results of the entire survey that is available to you at drdannybaer.blogspot.com.

The survey shows that 84 percent of Free Will Baptist churches practice feet washing. And they do so on average of 2 times per year.

75 percent of our pastors believe feet washing should be an ordinance. In the comment section there were some who indicated that they thought feet washing should be practiced – but not labeled as an ordinance. There were also those who said they believed that communion and feet washing were actually one ordinance.

What this means is the ordinance of the washing of the saints feet is alive and well in our ranks. I had many pastors who seemed to take objection for the survey, thinking that it was part of some effort to remove feet washing as an ordinance. To you I say first of all, I had no such intension – and second of all, you can breathe easy. With 75 percent of pastors and 84 percent of churches we have a 'super majority."

We will limit our discussion today with the three ordinances listed in our treatise.

*The second question that arises is "what is an ordinance, anyway?"*

I suppose I should first mention that we believe in ordinances, not sacraments, such as the Catholics and Episcopalians. To them, a "sacrament" is a ritual or ceremony whereby God imparts grace upon the doer. You may indeed get a "blessing" from being baptized, but baptism does not impart the saving grace it symbolizes.

Defining "ordinance" is difficult, especially given that the word is not used in Scripture to describe those ceremonies that we call ordinances.

I cannot take the time to go into the nuances of that debate.

Here is what I would like to do. We as Free Will Baptists agree that there are three ordinances. And, I believe that we can agree on some basic principles of an ordinance.

First, an ordinance was "ordained" or commanded by Jesus Christ.

Secondly, an ordinance was "practiced" by Christ.
Thirdly, an ordinance was "practiced" by the early church.

We can all agree on those three statements.

I also believe that we can agree on this:

An ordinance is a ceremony that has a spiritual significance, but that points to a deeper spiritual meaning, without which, the ordinance is meaningless.

Let's take baptism, for example.

A baptism is a wonderful service. It is always a thrill to see someone follow the Lord in what can be rightly called believer's baptism.

I'll never forget my own baptism – the baptism of my children! Baptismal services can be a highlight of a church experience.

However, baptism points to a much deeper spiritual truth – that the one who is being immersed has been united with Christ and has been buried with Him and has risen again with Him to "walk in the newness of life."

Without this deeper spiritual truth, the ritual of baptism is meaningless. If you baptize a sinner, all you have is a wet sinner!

If fact, it could be argued that without the deeper spiritual reality, the ceremony is dangerous lest that baptized sinner somehow thinks he is right with God because he got dunked!

A similar argument could be made for the Lord's Supper.

Some of the most worshipful service I have ever attended have been our time of Communion. They truly have meaning and purpose – to remember the death of our Lord and Savior.

However, consuming the bread and cup must represent the fact that we have indeed have accepted Him as our Lord and Savior – that His body was broken and His blood was shed for us!

Is it not the same for Feet Washing?

Some of the most precious times in our fellowship are during feet washing. When researching for this message I talked to my brother who reminded me of our grandfather – Papaw – as we called him. Papaw resisted participating in Feet Washing for quite some time – maybe because his feet stunk to high heaven! When he finally decided to join in he washed the feet of one of our deacons. When he was finished, my Papaw, who was 6 feet tall and an extremely quiet man in church, grabbed that deacon, who was barely over 5 feet tall, and carried him around the room! What a service!!!

However, as wonderful and humbling and special those times are, this ceremony must point to a deeper spiritual truth – to willingly and humbly serve others from a heart of love.

Jesus was not just telling these men to only set aside two times a year where they would get together and wash each other's clean feet

That's what we so, don't we? One of the worst times is when you are on the way to church and you think, "Oh

NO!!! We're having feet washing tonight, and I forgot to wash my feet – and put on clean socks!!! How embarrassing!"

We believe he was indeed instituting a ceremony – an ordinance here. However, He meant much more than that! He wanted these men to wash each other's feet on a regular basis. I can't help but think that when Matthew visited Nathanial, that Nathaniel did not just provide water, but got down on his knees and washed Matthew's feet!

Now, you naysayers can say – but we don't do that anymore! It would be ludicrous to wash the feet of a guest to our house.

I would agree. However, the spiritual meaning is voluntary, humble, loving service. How long has it been since you have willingly humbled yourself before anyone and served them?

***In other words, have you washed anyone's feet lately?***

If you are part of small minority of Free Will Baptist who do not see this as an ordinance, then I submit to you that John 13 is still in your Bible! The deeper spiritual truth is still here. Have you washed anyone's feet lately?

If you are one who of the vast majority of FWB who hold to feet washing as an ordinance, don't forget the deeper truth. The ceremony is not an end in itself!!!!
Have you washed anyone's feet lately?

By the way, for you who are from those churches please know this. According to my survey only about 34% of the adults who attend your churches participate in the ordinance.

I hope you can go home and preach this truth and increase that percentage.

But more than that, I hope that you can preach this truth and your people will begin looking for ways they can wash feet in their daily walk. You need to ask them:
Have you washed anyone's feet lately?

## III. A PRACTICAL EXAMPLE

In 1927, a 30 year old, unmarried Free Will Baptist women went to a mission service. She had to go to another denomination because there were no Free Will Baptist missionaries at that time.

At the end of the service she prayed that God would send workers to reach to lost souls abroad. At that point it was almost as if the Lord said to her, "Why don't you go?"

Her response was immediate. "I cannot go. Who would take care of Mother?"

You see, Bessie was the youngest of 11 children. It became her lot to take care of her aged mother, and she had done so for many years.

Also, Bessie knew that she needed training, and the idea of furthering her education seemed impossible.

That winter two things happened: Her mother passed away, and the Southern Ohio Bible Institute started just a few miles away in Portsmouth, Ohio. In 1932 she transferred to a Bible school run by the "Gospel Missionary Union" in Kansas City, Missouri now called "Avant Ministries."

In 1936, at the age of 40, Bessie Yeley stepped on a Dutch Steamship in New York and began the long journey to Venezuela for her first missionary appointment under Faith Baptist Mission – a contact she had made through another Bible college where she had transferred to in Kansas City, Missouri. She went out from her home church, Porter FWB mentioned earlier, and the Porter and Pine Creek Quarterly Conferences.

In 1938 she came under the FWB Foreign Mission department. At that time there were four missionaries – Miss Laura Bell Barnard in India, the Willeys in Panama, and Bessie Yeley in Venezuela.

In 1942, now 46 years of age, Bessie joined the Willies in their new work in Cuba. It has been my privilege to visit Cuba a number of times over the past few years. Each time I go I meet someone who remembers Miss Yeley, as they called her.

In 1955, now 59 Bessie returned to the states, primarily for health reasons. In 1956 she began serving on the border of

Mexico in Texas and Arizona on the border of Mexico. Following her ministry there she traveled to Miami to work with Cuban Refugees.

In 1965 she retired at the age of 69! But even then she moved to an apartment in the "Projects" in her home town of Portsmouth. She called it "just a change of work, nothing more." She spent the remainder of her years ministering to children and the elderly until she died in 1969 at the age of 73.

For 15 years of her teen and adult life, Bessie washed the feet of her Mother and the people of Porter Church where she taught Sunday school, kept the books, played the pump organ and carried out the ashes from the old stove in the middle of the sanctuary.

For 6 years she washed the feet of the Venezuelans.

For 13 years she washed the feet of the Cubans.

For 9 years she washed the feet of Mexicans and Cuban refugees.

For the last 5 years of her life she washed the feet of the poor and needy in her home town – until one day in January she died on a bus, alone.

Bessie Yeley gave her life in voluntary, humble loving service. She spent her life washing feet.

I have a copy of a number of documents concerning Bessie and copies of a number of letters she wrote — especially during that first year.

In a letter she penned on the Dutch steamship that she took from New York to Caracas, Venezuela. It is dated July 5th and written on the ship's letterhead.

In the letter she describes life on the boat — it was far from the cruise liners of our day!

On the last page, near the bottom she wrote these words, "So long and don't worry about me a minute for I am getting along just fine and am happy as can be."

*Have you washed anyone's feet lately?*

# 5

## CONTENDING FOR TRUE WORSHIP
### John 4:19-25
### Southeastern Conference
### Dr. Danny Baer

Let's do a word association: worship, What comes to your mind?

- Music
- Praise?
- Worship Service?
- Worship Leader?
- This Guy?
- Place Of Worship?
- Bowing/Kneeling?
- Praying?
- Obedience
- Devotion?
- Your Worship?? - (Magistrates And Mayors In Uk)

Truth is, there are many ideas, concepts and opinions concerning worship.

My message today is "Contending for True Worship"
Read verses: John 4:19-25

---

**Illustration:**

In March ....

My wife and I stood in Old San Juan.

San Juan Bautista Cathedral is named after Puerto Rico's patron saint (Saint John the Baptist) and is located in the heart of Old San Juan on Cristo Street (Calle del Cristo)

The original cathedral in what was the city of Puerto Rico (changed to San Juan after the Spanish-American War) was constructed from wood in 1521 -- almost a century before the settlement of Jamestown!!!

"Please remove your sunglasses and hats, for you are entering a place of worship."

I did -- out of respect.

---

"A place of worship."

I've been to many

> Hari Krishna temple -- the Palace of Gold -- Wheeling, WV
> St. Patrick's Cathedral -- Madison Ave, NY
> Duke Chapel -- where I sang in a wedding

---

Small white "Presbyterian" church at the base of Snow Shoe Mt.

"Don't drink the communion."

Barbecena, Brazil - Church of the Good Death -- Pope Francis chosen

There are many "places of worship"
By some counts between 300-350,000 in the US alone!

This is what this "woman at the well" wanted to know --
Jesus had centered in on her problem
She wanted to "change the subject" -- where do I worship???
Jesus said "in spirit and in truth"

This is one of the best passages in the N.T. == possibly the entire Bible about **worship**

**I. We Must Worship!**

At least the "Assumption" or "presumption" of worship here.

What is worship?

**English: Old English - Worth ship (English: "Worth Ship")**

When we worship we are somehow conveying to God -- to others -- to ourselves -- just how much God is worth to us!

God's worth!!! Imagine the thought!!!

How much is God worth to you???

How much do you value God??

Economics class:
How much is something worth -- how do you set a price?
Value added?
What competitors charge?
Price fixed??
An item is worth what someone is willing to pay for it!!!

An item is worth what someone is willing to pay for it!!!

Another Economics principle:
When you pay for something – the money is just a value holder.
What you are really paying is the blood, sweat and tears it took for you to earn that money!
What you are really paying is PART OF YOU!!!

BY THE WAY!!! TEACH TO THIS TO YOUR CHILDREN!!!

What is it really worth?
It's worth what you will pay for it!
How much you will give of yourself for it!!!

HOW MUCH DO YOU GIVE OF YOURSELF TO GOD???

HOW MUCH DO YOU GIVE OF YOUR OWN SWEAT, BLOOD AND TEARS TO GOD??

HOW MUCH SKIN DO YOU HAVE IN THE GAME???

We live in a day where people want worship with no skin in the game.

This is what we do sometimes:
We dress up on Sunday mornings. etc.
Throw some money in the plate.
Think we are doing God a favor.

This is contrary to Biblical worship!!
We cannot through God our leftovers
We cannot give out of our abundance
We cannot attend church if there's nothing else going on more important!

David knew the importance of valuing his service to God:
In 2 Samuel 24, after David has sinned regarding the numbering of Israel, we was told to build an altar and give sacrifice in "the threshing floor of Araunah the Jebusite."

Aruanah wanted to give the land to his king, but David said, "Nay; but I will surely buy [it] of thee at a price: neither will I offer burnt offerings unto the LORD my God of that which doth cost me nothing."

In the O.T. "Worship" is tied to singing at times.
However, often it is tied to <u>sacrifice.</u>

David, the sweet songster of Israel, knew the meaning of worship!

J. Oswald Chambers, in *My Utmost for His Highest* said,
"Worship is giving God the best that He has given you."

**Old Testament**

Hebrew word - **shachah - "Bow Down - prostrate oneself"**
**(Hebrew: "Bow Down")**
Worship - 100 times
Bow Down - 50 times

For Example:
In Gen 22:5 Abraham, when he took Isaac on the mountain to sacrifice him said, "I and the lad will go yonder and worship, and come again to you."

In Exodus 20 after we are given the second commandment not to make any graven images, God goes on to say, "Thou shalt not bow down thyself to them."

Same Hebrew word.

In the minds of the Hebrews, worship and lowering oneself before a holy God were synonymous.

I am lowly - you are lofty
I am weak - you are almighty
I am small - you are great

Compared to you, I am of no value!!! -- You have great value to me!!!!!!
You have worth! You are worthy! You should be worshiped.

**New Testament**

Greek word - **proskuneo -** to kiss the hand –
(Greek: "To Kiss the Hand")

-among the Orientals, expressly, the Persians; to fall upon the knees and touch the ground with the forehead as an expression of profound reverence

- in the NT by kneeling or prostration to do homage (to one) or make obeisance, whether in order to express respect or to make supplication

There is still the idea of "bowing" -- showing respect – obeisance.

However, there is the added element -- kissing the hand -- showing affection, adoration.

As with any spiritual truth,

The Old Testament emphasized the outward, the NT the inward
The OT the position of the body, the NT the condition of the heart
The OT - worship embodied in ritual

Jesus wanted to counter that!

Therefore, he said, ...

## II. We Must Worship in Spirit!

The "Woman" in the story wanted to pin Jesus in a corner.

She had just been confronted with her sin.

She wanted to know about the "place of worship."
    Her mind went what was probably an "automatic" response
        Not "how" do I get right with God.
        Not "how" do I approach God?
        But "where"

Jesus told her that it is not a "place"!!!

A "place" is physical - worship must be "in spirit"

Not tied to a place
    (True worship is not tied to a PLACE)
    By the way... we have all heard -- "I can worship God on the lake"
    Even though "worship" is not tied to a place -- I believe in the local church
        Acts 2:42
        Gospel - epistles ... Revelation

You cannot define NT Christianity without the local church
I believe in the local church
I understand the value of communal worship -- missing in our generation

HOWEVER!!!! We do not want our people to get the idea that the only place to "worship" is in a building!!!

Not tied to a physical movement
(True worship is not tied to the PHYSICAL)
We are guilty of trying to get people to shout or cry or clap or wave the hands.
Worship is not a position of the body!!!
Worship is a condition of the heart!!!!!!

We are emotional creatures
(True worship is not tied to our EMOTIONS)
Emotions will "result" from a heartfelt expression of adoration and love and gratefulness -- from the awesome realization in the depths of our soul of who God is and what he has done for us!!!

Worship is not dependent upon location, but devotion
Worship is not restricted by a physical action, but by a spiritual condition.
Worship does not result from an emotional state, but will result in a genuine emotional response

But Jesus did not end his discussion there.

### III. We Must Worship in Truth!

If worship was only tied to devotion
The Hari Krishna's on the mountain in WV would be worshiping
But they are not.. Their worship is based on a lie
The Whirling Dirvishes in Turkey would be worshiping
But they are not. Their worship is based on a lie.
Muslims around the world who follow the five pillars would be worshiping
But they are not. Their worship is based on a lie.
Catholics who take the mass == the body of Christ -- would be worshiping
But they are not. Their worship is based on a lie.

Is our worship based on the truth of God's word?

Even so called "Christian" churches are not immune.

It is alarming that even though many associate music with worship
Often our music is often biblically anemic
or worse -- scripturally wrong!!!

Our accolades often are for the praise of men not the praise of God!

"When we obey God, we're not doing it for God. I mean that's one way to look at it.

We're doing it for ourselves, because God takes pleasure when we're happy.

That's the thing that gives him the greatest joy this morning.

So I want you to know this morning, just do good for your own self.

Do good because God wants you to be happy.

When you come to church, when you worship Him, you're not doing it for God, really. You're doing it for yourself.

Because that's what makes God happy, amen? Let's open our hearts to Him today."

Notice what she said!

*When you come to church, when you worship Him, you're not doing it for God, really. You're doing it for yourself.*

A month later she said that she "did not mean to imply that we don't worship God."

However, her words were plain and her message clear.

If you bow before God or pray to Him or sing of Him, and your thought is "What can I get out of this?" YOU ARE NOT WORSHIPING GOD!!!

I'm happy that the fruit of the spirit includes "Joy." That is the result of surrendering to God... that is not the goal!

JOY AND HAPPINESS IS THE RESULT OF SURRENDING TO GOD
NOT THE GOAL OF SURRENDING TO GOD!

OUR MOTIVATION FOR WORSHIP MUST BE OUR LOVE FOR GOD AND OUR DESIRE TO SOMEHOW EXPRESS TO HIM HOW MUCH HE IS WORTH TO US!!!!

We need to worship Him in spirit and in truth!

**Conclusion**

So, how are we doing?

Are you involved in spiritual worship?
Do you measure your worship by your physical surroundings or position?

Is your worship based on the truth of the Word of God.

How much is God worth to you?

The next time you hear someone say, "Does a Christian have to tithe?"
The answer, "How much is God worth to you?"

Express in your giving how much God is worth to you!

Some of you spent more money at a restaurant than you put in the offering plate.

Spend more on the golf course than their weekly giving.

Spend more on a boat than on a building program.

HOW MUCH IS GOD REALLY WORTH TO THEM???

IT'S NOT ALL ABOUT MONEY ---

BUT THAT IS A PRETTY GOOD MEASURE OF WHAT WE VALUE!

The next time you are debating on whether to "spend your time" at church on Sunday or Wednesday night or in revival,

Ask, "How much is God really worth to me?"

When you are asked to work in the nursery or on a bus route,

How much is God worth to you?

Next time, you get discouraged and defeated and want to quit.

Ask, "How much is God worth to me?"

HE IS WORTH IT ALL!

HE IS WORTHY OF ALL OUR PRAISE.

HE IS WORTHY OF ME BECOMING A LIVING SACRIFICE!!!

"GOD, YOU ARE WORTH!!!!"

"GOD, YOU ARE WORTH ALL TO ME!!!!"

# 6

## Reasoning With God

Jason Jones
Sunday School Superintendent
Canaan Land, Grove City

Come now, and let us reason together, saith the Lord: though your sins be as scarlet, they shall be as white as snow; though they be red like crimson, they shall be as wool.

Isaiah 1:18

### White as snow:

As I read and studied this passage, it seemed increasingly odd to me at the first. It seemed odd, because this was a message to compel God's people toward Him. Per this world's wisdom, "Marketing 101" will tell you that if you want to compel someone to desire what you have to offer, you use items that will appeal to your audience. In this scripture, God uses snow… who in their right mind is appealed to by the thought of snow? This question forced me to look deeper into the text. So I studied snow. Here's what I found:

i.   Snow isn't actually white. Snow is a bunch of ice crystals grouped together. The snow crystals redirect light waves that pass through and onto other nearby crystals.

ii.   The "white" appearance of snow is the reflection (redirection) of "white" light.

iii.   If snow looks white, it's because we are actually seeing the color of the light that has been redirected through it.

As I considered these facts, I thought that maybe what God was trying to show us is that although our sins are stained red, when he gets done with us, we shall be clean spiritually to the point of these ice crystals. The Light of Jesus Christ is what makes us appear white. This can only happen if we are transparent with Christ about the sin in our life and repent from it. We should be able, as Christians, to redirect the "full color spectrum" of the Light of the world, and not just pick and choose what we like about the Bible, Christianity, or God.

**Wool:**

So I looked at the next analogy, and wondered about that one as well. It didn't make sense at first glance that God would choose wool to liken the final state of our sins.

i.   Wool isn't naturally white; while on sheep, it is actually an off-white (or dirty-white). Freshly sheared wool is known as "greasy wool".

ii. The sheep is sheared of its' wool before the wool is scoured.

iii. The wool is scoured in order to remove contaminants, and appear truly white.

So with this information, I thought that maybe God was showing us that like the sheep's wool, our sin must first be sheared from our hearts before He (the Shepherd) can scour it and remove the contaminates... making it truly white (and clean).

# 6

# A TESTIMONY TO THE FAITHFULNESS OF GOD

Text: 2 Timothy 4:1-18
Key verses: Verses 17, 18
Glen Poston, Tennessee
Homecoming message at
Canaan Free Will Baptist Church Creston

## Introduction

We are here today to celebrate nearly 30 years of God's faithfulness to this church. God has been faithful to you! He's blessed you! You have a great heritage. I believe God's faithfulness is the overwhelming theme of our text today.

Bible scholars believe this letter was most likely written to Timothy during Paul's second Roman imprisonment, later than the one recorded in Acts 28. It is believed that he was awaiting death at the hand of Nero and this is his last epistle. He was virtually alone in a Roman prison.
He knew that his work was done and his life was almost over. Notice verses 6 and 7 , "For I am now ready to be offered, and the time of my departure is at hand. I have fought a good fight; I have finished my course; I have kept the faith. It appears Paul was in a dungeon where he was

cold. In verse 13, he asked Timothy to bring his coat to him. He appears to be lonely and perhaps a little melancholy.

At least one of his co-workers had abandoned him. Others had been sent away to other duties. He said, Demas has forsaken me having loved this present world. (v.10). Crescens had left for Galacia and Titus to Dalmacia. (v.10). He also told Timothy how Alexander had done him wrong. (v.14). We're not sure but this might have been the same Alexander that Paul said in 1 Tim. 1:20 that he had turned over to Satan that he might learn not to blaspheme.

If you have ever been lonely, abandoned or in a terrible situation, then you should be able to identify with the Apostle Paul. In verse 16 he said, "At my first answer, no man stood with me but all men forsook me."

But, praise the Lord, look at verses 17 and 18. Paul pivots and proceeds to think on the faithfulness of God. Notice the word, **"Notwithstanding..."** Do you know what the word notwithstanding means? It means "**but...**" Have you ever noticed how "but" changes everything? Paul is just transitioning. Sure he's been cold! Sure he has experienced loneliness and desertion! Sure he's been hurt! Have you ever been hurt? We've all been hurt.

You know what we need to do when we've been hurt! **Get over it!** And so Paul begins to reflect on God's faithfulness. He says in verses 17 and 18... The Lord stood with me. The Lord strengthened me. The Lord shall deliver me. (ESV The Lord will **rescue** me.). The Lord will preserve me unto His heavenly kingdom. (ESV He will **bring me safely** into his heavenly kingdom.)

***Propositional Statement: We Serve A Faithful God and He can always be trusted to stand with us, strengthen us, deliver us and bring us safely into His heavenly kingdom.***

There are Christians today who are wringing their hands about the shape the world is in. They are worried to death about this election. Many are worried about both candidates. They are worried about who will be appointed to the Supreme Court. Now listen. I know there is plenty of room to be concerned and we ought to be but what we ought to do is exactly what Paul did in his situation and that is reflect on the faithfulness of God.

I.    **First, The Lord Is Faithful To Stand With Us  (verse 17)**
Paul said, "the Lord stood with me." What does it mean to stand with someone?  The Greek word used here is *par-is-tay-mee* and it carries the idea of standing beside, ready to give aid. I am reminded of what David said in Psalms 46:1 "God is our refuge and strength, a **very present help** in trouble." Sometimes our earthly friends let us down. They leave us or forsake us.

Jesus said, "I will never leave you or forsake you." People in general often let us down. Sometimes even our fathers and mothers can let us down. <u>But the Lord will stand with you.</u>  Maybe you've been let down by a friend. Maybe you've been let down by a pastor. There are probably some of you here who have been let down by a spouse, Listen to me, Jesus won't let you down.

**Illustration** As his UCLA football team suffered through a poor season in the early 1970's, head coach **Pepper Rodgers** came under intense criticism and pressure from alumni and fans. Things got so bad, he remembers that friends became hard to find. "My dog was my only true friend," Rodgers said of that year. **"I told my wife that every man needs at least two good friends. So she bought me another dog."**

**Illustration:** The wealthy, eccentric **Howard Hughes**, at the time had a wealth amassed of over four billion dollars said, **"I'd give it all for one good friend."**

Oh dear brothers and sisters we need to learn what Paul had learned, "What a friend we have in Jesus! He will stand with you. After the children of Israel wandered in the wilderness for 40 years, God spoke to Joshua in chapter 1, verse 5. He said, "Have not I commanded thee? Be strong and of a good courage; be not afraid, neither be thou dismayed: for the Lord thy God is with thee whithersoever thou goest.

- In the book of Haggai, after the temple had been destroyed after the Babylonian captivity, God wanted His temple to be rebuilt. He sent his prophet Haggai to the people in chapter 1:13, "Then spake Haggai the Lord's messenger in the Lord's message unto the people, saying,

I am **with** you, saith the Lord. And then again in Haggai 2:4 "Yet now be strong, O Zerubbabel, saith the Lord; and be strong, O Joshua, son of Josedech, the high priest; and be strong, all ye people of the land, saith the Lord, and work: for I am with you, saith the Lord of hosts: But I also want you to see what else Paul said in our text.......He said......

## II. Secondly, The Lord Is Faithful To Strengthen Us

Vines Expository Dictionary of New Testament Words says that the word used here for strengthen implies inward strength suggesting strength in soul and purpose. I have found that what the Lord calls you to do, He will always give you the strength to accomplish it. Paul tells us the purpose for which God strengthened him in verse 17, "That by me the preaching shall be fully known and that all the Gentiles might hear."

Have you ever noticed that God does not usually give us the strength we need until the time that we need it. What the Lord has for you to endure, he will give you the strength to endure it.

*If I asked you if you could bare losing a child or a grandchild, you would say, "No, absolutely not, I don't think I could bare losing my child or grandchild."*

*Now obviously I pray none of you ever have to go through that but God can be trusted to strengthen us when we need it.*

In Isaiah 40:29, the Bible says, "He giveth power to the faint, and to them that have no might He increaseth strength." In 2 Corinthians 1:8-10 Paul told the Corinthians, "For we would not have you ignorant, brethren, of our trouble which came to us in Asia: that we were pressed out of measure, beyond strength, insomuch that we despaired even of life. But we had the sentence of death in ourselves that we should not trust in ourselves but in God who raiseth the dead..." In 2 Corinthians 12:9, Paul said that God told him, "My grace is sufficient for thee, for My strength is made perfect in weakness. Most gladly therefore will I glory rather in my infirmities, that the power of Christ may rest upon me."

Let me remind you where Paul was. We can't say for sure but many scholars believe he was in the Mamertine Prison and they say the stench would be inconceivable. There was no sanitation, or clean water. It was a filthy, vile, wretched place...cold, dark, damp and yet here Paul says, "God stood with me and strengthened me."

### III. Thirdly, The Lord Is Faithful To Deliver Us.

In verse 17 Paul said God had delivered him from the mouth of the lion and in verse 18 he said God would deliver him from every evil work." The idea is that when we are forsaken, lonely and troubled, the Good Lord will rescue us. Paul said he was delivered out of the mouth of the lion. Perhaps he was talking literally. Nero the emperor was known to toss Christians into the arena filled with lions just for sport. He also was known to light his gardens by burning Christians at the stake. It could have been literal.

Maybe it was a figure of speech. Paul, in another place, says that Satan is like a roaring lion seeking whom he may devour. Ever felt like Satan was wanting to eat you up. Hey, he does! David went before a cowardly King Saul and let him know that he was willing to fight the Philistine giant, Goliath. In I Samuel 17:37, "David said moreover, The Lord that delivered me out of the paw of the lion, and out of the paw of the bear, he will deliver me out of the hand of this Philistine. And Saul said unto David, Go, and the Lord be with thee."

The idea of God's deliverance and rescuing is repeatedly used by David in the Psalms. Just to mention a few reference in Ps. 18:
Verse 2 - "The Lord is my rock, my fortress, my deliverer."
Verse 17 - "He delivered me from my strong enemy and from them who had me."
Verse 43 - "Thou hast delivered me from the strivings of the people."
Verse 48 - "He delivered me from my enemies."

Yes, dear brothers and sisters the Lord knows how to rescue you. He's rescued me so many times I can hardly count them. He can deliver you from **financial** trouble. He can deliver you when your **marriage** is in trouble. He can deliver you when you **lose your job** or your **health.**
Now I didn't say you would never have problems. I said he could deliver you and rescue you

Daniel and the three Hebrew children are good examples. God delivered them from the fiery furnace.

Now in this particular instance, it is believed that God chose to rescue Paul permanently by taking him on to Heaven.

It is believed that Paul was beheaded shortly after finishing this letter but I remind you that Paul seemed to know this was about to happen. Look at verse 6 "For I am now ready to be offered, and the time of my departure is at hand."

Sometimes God delivers us temporarily and one day He will deliver us permanently. Most of us do not have the privilege to know when its temporary or when its permanent like Paul seemed to know.
You say, "Oh preacher, that's a cop out." to say the Lord will deliver us permanently by taking us to Heaven.

**Illustration:** Last Saturday I did the graveside service for Mrs. Virginia Smith. If there ever was a saint, it was Miss Ginny. She had lost her husband over 20 years ago. Her body was wracked with pain. She had asked me several years ago if I would do her graveside funeral in Tennessee. She had moved to Alabama to be near her only daughter and granddaughter. I heard she was near death. Do you know what I prayed? I prayed, "Lord, will you please deliver Miss Ginny from all this suffering and take her on to Heaven." None of us are going to get out of this world alive, it's not a cop out to say, and sometimes the Lord delivers us by taking us on to Heaven.

- Paul was ready to go. He said in verses 6 and 7, "I am ready to be offered... my departure is at hand...I have fought a good fight...I have finished my course!"

- **Illustration:** I remember visiting with my dear friend Brother Howard Munsey towards the end of his bout with cancer. As I prayed with him just a short time before his death, he told me. "My cancer is bad. I may die soon or the Lord can perform a miracle if He wants to. And then he said something I'll never forget. He said, "It doesn't really matter to me either way."

## IV. Finally, The Lord Is Faithful To Preserve Us.

What does preserve mean? It means to maintain, keep alive and retain. What do we need to do to maintain? We need to do the same things Paul told Timothy in the beginning of this chapter in verses 2-5. He said: Keep on preaching the Word. Be instant in season and out of season (it is out of season now for sure). Reprove, rebuke and exhort with all long-suffering (keep encouraging people and be patient with them). Watch in all things (that means be sober minded)

1. Endure afflictions
2. Do the work of an evangelist
3. Make full proof of our ministry.

The KJV says, "He will preserve me unto his heavenly kingdom. I also like the way the way another translation puts it. (ESV) He will bring me safely into His heavenly kingdom." Listen God is able to keep you and preserve you. I'm not trying to be humble or down on myself but I'm here to tell you there is not that much that is amazing about Glenn Poston. The only amazing thing about Glenn Poston is that he's still here and he is still in the race and I know it is only because the Lord has kept me. He has preserved me. He's kept me spiritually and he's kept me physically. He's helped me through hard times and discouraging times. He's helped me when I was weak and when I wanted to quit. Paul recognized that the prophecy God revealed about him on the road to Damascus was true.

God told Ananias in Acts 9:15-16, **15** But the Lord said unto him, "Go thy way, for he is a chosen vessel unto Me, to bear My name before the Gentiles and kings and the children of Israel. The Lord preserved Paul. Read about all the things he suffered —shipwreck, bitten by poisonous snakes, stoned and left for dead, deserted by his friends— You name it, Paul endured hardship. And yet he says, "The Lord delivered me and the Lord will deliver me and will bring me safely to His heavenly Kingdom." Paul is talking here about eternal glory. In spite of all of our difficulties, in spite of loneliness, in spite of deprivation, in spite of pain, in spite of anything we may go through, even the executioners axe,  if we keep our trust in the Lord, He will bring us to His heavenly kingdom. Physical death does not keep us from entering His heavenly kingdom. **In fact, it is the door which will ultimately usher us into the heavenly kingdom**. And for that we can say, Glory!

## Conclusion

Why does God stand with us, strengthen us, deliver and rescue us, and preserve us? He does it so that we can fulfill the purpose for which He saved us for.

In verse 17, Paul says, "the Lord stood by me and strengthened me — that by me the preaching might be fully known and that all the Gentiles might hear." Paul was known as the Apostle to the Gentiles. Aren't you glad Paul was faithful to his calling?

Listen to me, this church has a purpose and we all have a purpose. God equips all of us with different gifts. Somewhere American Christianity got it in their minds that the only reason God saved us was so that we can go to Heaven when we die and we can enjoy life down here. Don't get me wrong, I do want to go to Heaven when I die and I do believe that we can enjoy life down here— but we were made for a greater purpose than drinking coffee and enjoying pot-luck suppers. Rejoice today in God's goodness but be faithful to fulfill God's purpose in your life.

Rejoice in your salvation but be faithful to fulfill your purpose. Be glad that He will stand with you, strengthen you, deliver you and preserve you. But let's stay busy fulfilling God's purpose in our lives.

# 7

## Be Kind

### Scripture: Ephesians 4:31-32

June 25, 2016
Ohio State Association of Free Will Baptist Meeting
Mike Martin
Calvary FWB, Ravenna

I'm thankful to Bro. Edwin and the board to invite me to lead in our devotions this morning.

I have a Warren Wiersbe inspired title for this devotion: "Be Kind" and we will be in Ephesians 4

I want to begin with a quote from one of my favorite writers.

Though I didn't have the pleasure of knowing him personally, I came to love him and his "Briefcase" and was happy to finally meet him at the National in 2009.

Bro. Jack Williams passed away on April 29 this year.

Bro Jack was a very kind and encouraging man. After publishing an article in Contact by a 26 year old East Tennessee pastor, they encouraged that pastor to pursue writing. Now, he has a blog on the Huffington post and many of our churches are reading and distributing his book called "Simple"!

In his tribute article to Bro. Jack, Eric Thomsen offered a collection of a few of Cowboy Jack's best moments, one of which was:

**"The best of us are difficult sometimes; the rest of us are difficult more frequently."**

(April/May 2005 One Magazine http://www.onemag.org/small_cowboy.htm)

Regrettably, I often fall into the latter category.

Sometimes it can be too easy to become difficult if we are not careful, whether driving, ordering fast food, or talking with customer service or tech support

And what's worse...my children too often witness my anger and frustration, instead of my patience and kindness.

The first four of the Ten Commandments teach us to Love God by putting Him first, turning away from idolatry, honoring His name and remembering the Sabbath.

The last six of the Ten Commandments teach us to Love Others by honoring our parents, life, purity, property, truth, and taking control of the thoughts and intents of our mind and heart.

Jesus summed up these 10 commandments into the 2 greatest commandments, to love God and love others.

In regards to loving others, Paul tells us in

*Ephesians 4:31-32 31 Let all bitterness, and wrath, and anger, and clamour, and evil speaking, be put away from you, with all malice: 32 And be ye kind one to another, tenderhearted, forgiving one another, even as God for Christ's sake hath forgiven you.*

We MUST determine this morning to show more kindness...

### 1) Pray for those who are difficult and unkind

Job prayed for his friends

*Job 42:10 KJV And the LORD turned the captivity of Job, when he prayed for his friends: also the LORD gave Job twice as much as he had before.*

Matthew Henry

*"God is better served and pleased with our warm devotions than with our warm disputations."* (Matthew Henry's Commentary on Job 42:10)

### 2) Speak the truth in love

*Ephesians 4:15 But speaking the truth in love, may grow up into him in all things, which is the head, even Christ:*

If you're like me, speaking the truth is the easy part. Tempering that truth with love can be difficult.

Matthew Henry

*"Christians should endeavour to promote a useful conversation: that it may minister grace unto the hearers; that it may be good for, and acceptable to, the hearers, in the way of information, counsel, pertinent reproof, or the like. Observe, It is the great duty of Christians to take care that they offend not with their lips, and that they improve discourse and converse, as much as may be, for the good of others."*

(Matthew Henry's Commentary on Ephesians 4:29)

*"Bitterness, wrath, anger"* defined by Henry as *"violent inward resentment and displeasure against others"*

(Matthew Henry's Commentary on Ephesians 4:31,32)

*"Kind one to another"* Henry says *"implies the principle of love in the heart, and the outward expressions of it, in an affable, humble, courteous behaviour."*

(Matthew Henry's Commentary on Ephesians 4:31,32)

### 3) **Don't allow your desire to correct someone prevent kindness**

*1 Samuel 25:3 "...Abigail...was a woman of good understanding..."*

Abigails husband on the other hand, well, let's just say if Abigail wore a shirt that said "I'm with stupid" it would be quite accurate.

*1 Sam 25:25 "for as his name is, so is he; Nabal is his name, and folly is with him:"*

She took matters into her own hands and prevented a great slaughter while saving David from the bitterness of revenge that otherwise would have been upon his conscience.

David responded to her

*1 Samuel 25:33 KJV And blessed be thy advice, and blessed be thou, which hast kept me this day from coming to shed blood, and from avenging myself with mine own hand.*

That day, David was convinced that showing kindness to Nabal was better.

I wonder what it might take today, to convince the church that kindness is the way to go?

That we will not reach the lost with **bitterness, wrath, anger, clamour, evil speaking,**

The last 6 commandments lead us to be kind with those around us.

As the church, we MUST show kindness, not just to the household of faith, but to those outside the church as well.

Now, you might be thinking, "I'm a pretty kind person"

Let me just add, kindness is not always best defined by you.

4) **Consider what others think is kind (or not),**

As author and radio host Dennis Prager said:

*We show love to those we love by doing what they consider loving, not necessarily by what we consider loving.*

(http://www.dennisprager.com/some-thoughts-on-love/)

A young man was not planning to give his girlfriend flowers or even a card, or to do anything special for her on Valentine's Day. His reason was that he considered Valentine's Day a creation of American capitalism — just another way to sell cards, flowers and gift items and increase companies' profits.

However, his girlfriend thought it important that he do something special for her on Valentine's Day.

Then he was asked if he considered birthdays special and expected his girlfriend to do or get something special for him on his birthday. He said he did.

So how would he react if his girlfriend dismissed the significance of birthdays the way he dismissed the importance of Valentine's Day and ignored his birthday? He acknowledged that he would be hurt.

Just as his girlfriend should make his birthday special whether or not she believes in the importance of birthdays, he should make Valentine's Day special for her whether or not he deems the day special.

We show love to the other in the way he or she understands it, not the way we do.

Maybe you think you spoke the truth with love.

But the other person doesn't think that you did.

Perhaps you didn't.

Is there anyone you have bitterness against this morning?

Pray for them, speak the truth in love to them, but don't allow your desire to correct someone prevent that kindness, and in doing so, consider what others think is kind (or not kind).

*"The best of us are difficult sometimes; the rest of us are difficult more frequently."*

Let us strive to be less difficult and more kind as the Ten Commandments teaches and God expects.

And perhaps, as David Crowe said last night:

"If the world sees us obeying the commandments, it might change something."

# 8

# BEHOLD THE LAMB PREPARED
Luke 1 :26-38
Mike Blanton
Full-Time Evangelist
Grove City

**Intro**:  Way back in the dawn of time, man violated a sacred trust and fell into sin.  At that time, God promised man that there would come One Who would balance the scales, defeat evil and deliver humanity.  For thousands of years men waited.  And while men waited, God worked.

I.  v. 26-28 **THE PLACE RESERVED FOR THIS PREPARATION**

A. **It Was A Pure Place** – We are told that the angel came to "*a virgin*

I certainly do not understand all the mechanics of how God sent His Son into the world through the womb of a virgin, but I do know that the virgin birth of Jesus is a foundational doctrine of the Christian faith.  Without a virgin birth, we do not have a Savior.  Without a virgin birth, we have no hope.  Without a virgin birth, we have no foundation upon which to build the house of our faith!  To deny the virgin birth of Jesus is to deny Christ.

B. **It Was A Prophesied Place** –          Bethlehem

C. **It Was A Prepared Place** – To watch Mary as these verses unfold is to see a young woman who has been prepared for this moment.  History tells us that every faithful Jewish girl was looking for the messiah.  We are also told that every Jewish girl hoped that she would be the vessel chosen through which God would send His Messiah into the world.

Imagine the faith required for Mary to respond to the Lord as she did.  For a young unmarried woman to become pregnant in that day was to be the focus of shame, disgrace and a possible death sentence.  But, Mary was willing to bear the shame and the burden of being the vessel through which God would send His Son into the world.

Thank God for people like Mary who are willing to do all the Lord requires, regardless of what it may require of them.  May the Lord find a heart like that beating within every one of our chests! After all, nothing reveals our love for Jesus like our unquestioning obedience to all He requests of us, **John 14:15, 21**!

## II.   v. 29-33 **THE PROMISE REVEALED IN THIS PREPARATION**

A. v. 31, 32 **The Promise Of A Special Child** – Mary is told that she will become the mother of a son, but that this Son will be no ordinary child. He will be her son, therefore, He will be a human; but He will also be the "***Son of the Highest***." He will be a man, but He will also be God.   This was the prophecy of Isaiah, **Isa. 7:14**.

B. v. 31 **The Promise Of A Saving Child** – Mary is told that the child's name is to be "***Jesus***." This name was a common name in that day.   In the Hebrew tongue, it was the name "***Joshua***". Many Jewish parents named their male children Joshua, or as the Greeks rendered it, Jesus.   Of course, while the name might be common, the child to Whom it was given was not.

The name "***Jesus***" means "***Jehovah is Salvation***." Although Mary did not understand all that she was being told, she hears for the first time that Name which is above every name! She does not understand it now, but the child she will name Jesus will grow up and one day He will die on a cross to save lost sinners from their sins. He will be the only hope lost sinners have, **John 14:6**. His

Name will be the only Name that will open the gates of Heaven; redeem the human soul from the bondage of sin; deliver lost men from the threat of Hell; and speak peace and hope to those who do not know God. He would die on a cross; rise from the dead and ascend back into Heaven to guarantee salvation for all who would trust Him by faith. Thank God for the day God sent His Son into the world to be the Savior of God's people,

C. v. 32-33 **The Promise Of A Sovereign Child** – Mary is also told that this special child, this saving child would also be a sovereign child. She is told that He would be a sovereign with a special pedigree.

III. v. 34-38 **THE POWER RELEASED IN THIS PREPARATION**

A. v. 34-38 **The Power To Conquer Our Doubts** – Mary hears the words of the angel, but she confesses that she does not understand how this can happen. She, like all other Jews, expected the Messiah to enter the world by the old fashioned way. She wonders how she will be able to have a child, since she has never physically been with a man. To Mary's mind this is a dilemma that cannot be surmounted. Thankfully, the angel has the answer! He tells her that she is about to be part of the greatest miracle the world has ever known. God is about to turn Mary into a miracle!

The angel speaks the words that conquer Mary's doubts.

B. v. 35-38 **The Power To Carry Out His Desires** – The angel addresses *Mary's problem* by giving her a *promise*, **v. 35**; offering her some *proof,* **v. 36**; and by declaring God's *power*, **v. 37**. Mary is told that God is well able to do all the things He has said He will do. Gabriel declares the awesome power of God and offers hope and comfort for the heart of Mary.

# 9

## THE LAMB IS PROMISED
Genesis 3:1-21
Mike Blanton
Full-time evangelist
Grove City

## I. THE PERSONALITY OF THE PROMISED LAMB

A. **This Lamb Is Unique In His Origin** – We are told that this One Who is coming will the "***the seed of the woman***." This is a strange statement because by God's very design the "***seed***" is provided by the male members of every species. Here, we are told that the woman will produce an offspring without the aid of a man. This verse gives us the first kernel of a great truth that will be more fully revealed down the road. This verse is the first prophecy of the Virgin birth of the Lord Jesus Christ.

Satan did not understand it, Adam and Eve did not understand it; but God indicates that He will send His Lamb into the world through a woman without the involvement of a man! Of course, we know this is how the birth of Jesus came about. Isaiah prophesied it, **Isa. 7:14**; and the angel Gabriel announced it to Mary, **Luke 1:26-35**, and to Joseph, **Matt. 1:18-25**.

B. **This Lamb Is Unique In His Occupation** – This Lamb was coming into the world to do battle with the forces of evil. We are told that He was coming to "*bruise*" the serpent's head. This refers to a fatal injury. This Lamb was coming to this world not to show men a better way to live. He was not coming to improve their environment. He was not coming to improve their social standing. He was coming to defeat evil. That was His sole mission, **John 18:37; Heb. 2:14**. This promised One was coming to deliver humanity from the sin into which it had just fallen. Many men and women would battle evil over the years; this One would deal it a death blow. He was coming to do for men that which they could never do for themselves. He was coming to secure their liberty and salvation from sin.

II. **THE PURPOSE OF THE PROMISED LAMB**

A. **He Would Come As A Warrior** – The word "*enmity*" means "*hatred or enemy*." Of course, it brings to mind the natural hatred humans have for serpents, but there is much more in view here. The enmity or hatred referred to here runs far deeper than that of a man hating a snake. It refers to the hatred Satan possesses toward the Lord and all that the Lord represents. It refers to the hatred that resided within the heart of the devil that caused him to attack Adam and Eve in the Garden and tempt them to sin. It is a hatred that desires nothing less than the overthrow of the Lord and His kingdom. It is a hatred that demands the death of God and the installation of Satan as god, **Isa. 14:12-16; Eze. 28:11-19**. This is the battle that was raging in Eden! It had less to do with mankind than it did with Satan's desire to wage war on God Almighty.

Of course, Jesus did just that! From the instant this prophecy was given in **Genesis 3:15** until the moment Jesus Christ died on the cross and rose again from the dead; Satan did everything in his power to stop "*the seed of the woman*" from being born. He worked through Cain to kill Abel, **Gen. 4**. He sought to corrupt the human blood line through evil marriages, **Gen. 6**. He tried to kill the people of Israel in Egypt, **Ex. 1-2**. He tried to bring about their destruction by leading them into gross idolatry during the kingdom years of Israel.

B. **He Would Come As A Winner** – The serpent is told that he will "***bruise the heel***" of the seed of the woman, but the seed of the woman will "***bruise***" the head of the serpent. Bruising the heel refers to an injury that is not fatal; while bruising the head refers to a fatal wound. The word "***bruise***" has the idea of "***crushing or striking.***" The serpent might strike the heel of the coming Lamb, but the Lamb would crush the head of the serpent.

Of course, this was fulfilled at the cross. The Lamb of God endured death for God's elect, but death could not hold Him! On the third morning, He arose from the dead as the Victor in the greatest battle ever waged. But, in His dying and rising again, He inflicted a mortal would upon the head of the serpent that will ultimately end with him sentenced to an eternity in the Lake of Fire, **Rev. 20:10**.

III.   **THE PORTRAIT OF THE PROMISED LAMB** v. 21

A. **It Is A Portrait Of Sacrifice** – Imagine the horror that must have filled the hearts of Adam and Eve as they witnessed death for the very first time! They had never seen blood before, now they watch as God, with His Own hands, slaughters an animal to provide a covering for their nakedness. It was in that instant that they saw firsthand just how much their sin really cost. They finally understood that the wages of sin is death, **Gen. 2:17, Rom. 6:23**.

Now, understand that everything He went through; every stripe on His back; every agony He suffered; every disgrace He endured; everything He suffered during His life, His trial and His death was because of your sins! He was marred for you, **Isa. 52:14**. He bled for you. He died for you, **Isa. 53:4-6**!

B. **It Is A Portrait Of Sufficiency** – After Adam and Eve sinned and became aware of their nakedness, they attempted to cover themselves by making aprons of fig leaves. But, their efforts were insufficient and God killed an innocent animal to provide a covering for their bodies. God wanted to show them, and us, that the works of the flesh can never atone for, or cover, sin. It requires the death of the innocent in the place of the guilty. Sin is taken away only through the shedding of innocent blood, **Heb. 9:22**.

The whole point is this: you can try anything you please, whether it is religion, good works, clean living, etc., to please the Lord; but, nothing will be sufficient to deal with your sin problem, until you come to Jesus and are saved by grace. Then, and only then, can you stand before the Lord and be accepted by Him,

**Eph. 1:6**! Only Jesus Christ and His shed blood is sufficient to allow us to stand in His presence, **John 1:29**.

# 10

## BEHOLD THE LAMB PROVIDED
Luke 2:1-20
Mike Blanton
Full-time evangelist
Grove City

As the Lord gives liberty this morning, I want to preach on the subject, *Behold The Lamb Provided*. I want to tell you how and why God sent His Son Jesus into this world and what His birth can and does mean for you. Allow me to share three aspects of the Lamb's provision with you as we *Behold The Lamb Provided*.

I.  v. 1-7  **THE PLACE INVOLVED IN THE LAMB'S PROVISION**

    A. v. 4 **The Planning Of That Place** – The fact that Jesus was born in Bethlehem was no accident. It was predicted years before it came to pass, **Micah 5:2**. This was common knowledge among those who studied and knew the Scriptures, **Matt. 2:1-6**.

B. v. 1-6 **The Providence Of That Place** – While it should not surprise us that Jesus was born where the Bible says He would be, the events surrounding His arrival there are amazing. **Verse 4** tells us that Mary and Joseph lived in Nazareth. This city is some 70 miles north of Bethlehem.

C. v. 7 **The Poverty Of That Place** – We are told that the Savior's entrance into this world was anything but glorious. When the young couple arrived in Bethlehem, they discovered that there was no place for them to stay. They found refuge in a stall used to house animals. When Mary delivered Jesus, she placed the Baby in a feed trough.

*"form of a servant,"* **Phil. 2:5-8**.

The God Who made everything and Who could have had anything, chose to live a life of poverty. Why? There is just one answer: because He loves us! Listen to **2 Cor. 8:9**, *"**For ye know the grace of our Lord Jesus Christ, that, though he was rich, yet for your sakes he became poor, that ye through his poverty might be rich**"*

D. v. 7 **The Pictures Of That Place** – We are told that Mary took her baby and wrapped Him in *"swaddling clothes."* Then, we are told that she took the Baby and placed Him in a *"manger."* He came to satisfy the hungry souls of dying men. Therefore, it was appropriate that

Jesus was born in Bethlehem, which means "*The house of bread*" and that He was laid in a manger!

E. v. 7 **The Promise Of That Place** – I am glad that Jesus was born in a manger and not a palace. I am glad that He was born into humble surroundings and not into the opulence of wealth. Why? If He had been born in a palace, the shepherds we will talk about in a moment would not have had access to Him. But, because He was born in poverty and in humble surroundings, He is more approachable to the common man. You and I would feel uncomfortable approaching a Savior reared in the lap of luxury; but we have less trouble coming to a Lord who has walked some of the same hard paths we walk.

II. v. 8, 15-19 **THE PEOPLE INVOLVED IN THE LAMB'S PROVISION**

A. v. 8 **Their Occupation** – The Bible simply calls them "*shepherds.*"

Ill. What a blessing! Men may not care about you. People may look down on you in disgust because of who you are or because of what you have done in life. But, there is a God in Heaven Who loves you in spite of everything. There is a God Who desires to save you, if you will only come to Him! I sure am glad today that the Lord did not hold my past against me!

B. v. 15-16 **Their Obedience** – As soon as these men hear the news of the Savior's birth, they leave their sheep on the hillsides and run into the town of Bethlehem to find the Lord Jesus. When they arrive, they find everything to be just as the angels had said. What a picture of grace!

C. v. 17-19 **Their Obligation** – As soon as they realize the magnitude of the things they have experienced, they begin to share the news with all they meet. They tell everyone about the Baby in the manger Who is Christ the Lord. Of course, the people who hear them are astonished to hear shepherds talking about such spiritual matters, but I like to think that some heeded the message and went to see for themselves.

One of the blessings of the Gospel of grace is that it is too good to keep quiet about. As soon as you experience its power, you want others to experience it also.

III. v. 9-14; 20 **THE PRAISE INVOLVED IN THE LAMB'S PROVISION**

A. v. 9-14 **There Was Heavenly Praise** – As those shepherds go about the business of another boring night with their flocks, something astonishing takes place. There is the appearance of a heavenly entourage, bearing the good news that heaven has invaded earth, and that nothing would ever be the same again.

1. v. 9 **The Heavenly Appearance** –

2. v. 10-12 **The Heavenly Announcement** –
   What an announcement! The world had wallowed in the grip of sin for thousands of years; waiting for the appearance of One Who would sever the bonds of sin and deliver men from the curse. Now, He has come! The wait is over! Salvation will be accomplished, just as God had promised it would! And the announcement was made to those humble shepherds going about the ordinary business of life! You will notice that the angel made the message personal to the shepherds, "***unto you is born***," **v. 11**. Thank God the message is a personal one! It was given to those shepherds, but it was made available to all, **Rev. 22:17**.

3. v. 13-14 **The Heavenly Anthem** – As soon as this angel finishes delivering Heaven's message to the shepherds, he is joined by a great multitude of angels who praise God and declare the truth that the message is indeed for all men!

B.  v. 20 **There Was Human Praise** – After the shepherds hear the message and meet the Master, they return to their flocks rejoicing as they go. Their voices are also lifted up to God in Heaven to praise Him for His glorious gift.  But, notice the difference between their praise and the praise of the angels.  The angels praise the Lord for what He has done for others, **v. 11**.  The shepherds praise the Lord for what He has done for them, **v. 20**!  There is a difference.  I am glad you are saved and for all that the Lord has done for you; but I sure am glad the Lord has done something in my heart for which I can praise Him as well!)

1. **The Praise Of Convinced Hearts** – When they heard the message, no doubt those shepherds were amazed and maybe a little skeptical as well.  But, when they found Jesus, just as the angels said they would; when they met Him for themselves, they could praise Him from a heart that has been convinced of the truth!

2. **The Praise Of Changed Hearts** – It must have been something to watch a group of raw-boned, rough shepherds leave that town rejoicing and praising the name of the Lord.

Ill. That is what meeting Jesus will do for you!  He may not make you shout, at least in this life, but He will change you, **2 Cor. 5:17**. He will give you a new life and new way of life to go with it!  When He comes in, He changes everything!  And when He does, there will be some excitement about it.  There will be some joy.  After all, when He saves your souls, He changes you and fills you with *"joy unspeakable and full of glory,"* **1 Pet. 1:8**. Surely, some of that will leak out from time to time!  When Jesus takes you, saves you and changes you, you will want to praise Him for Who He is and what He has done in your life!

# 11

## HEAVEN
Job 14:14, "If a man die, shall he live again?"
Alton Loveless
Writer, Author, Publisher, Preacher

**Introduction:**
Terry Toler, a few years ago wrote the popular song, *JUST THINKING ABOUT HOME.* Another writer also wrote, *JUST GOING HOME.*

---

Years ago I decided with this satisfaction.
I would live my life as if he was coming for me.
--Even if he didn't.
Than to live as if I didn't believe he was coming, but to find out--He did!

---

Another rule that I have practiced for many years is: *I do not criticize another sin just because it's different that my own.*

Beliefs of the past:

- Pharods-Pyramids
- Babylonians and Assyrians – Road signs in Heaven. They believed a large cavern exists.
- Greek philosophers- Socrates and Plato argued for the indestuctibity of the soul.
- Aztecs-Toltecs-Incas record a belief in a hereafter.

Notice some of the songs we sing on the subject of heaven:

1. *Above the Bright Blue,*
2. *An Empty Mansion,*
3. *Heaven Holds All to Me,*
4. *Home of the Soul,*
5. *How beautiful Heaven Must Be,*
6. *Just Over in the Glory Land,*
7. *No Tears in Heaven,*
8. *They Tell Me of a Home,*
9. *Sing to Me of Heaven,*
10. *This World is Not My Home,*
11. *To Canaan's Land,*
12. *When We all Get to Heaven,*
13. *Won't it Be Wonderful There* and many others.

These all describe a place we should want to go.

There are two passages of Scripture touching the question before us. The first contains the words of Jesus Christ, "Verily, verily, I say unto thee, except a man be born again, he cannot see the kingdom of God." The second passage is recorded in Hebrews 12:14, "Follow peace with all men and holiness without which no man shall see the Lord;" that is to enjoy Him here and eternally.

**HEAVEN IS REAL because it was,**
DESIGNED BY GOD:

> 1 COR. 2:9 But as it is written, Eye hath not seen, nor ear heard, neither have entered into the heart of man, the things which God hath prepared for them that love him.

> Job 19:25 For I know that my redeemer liveth, and that he shall stand at the latter day upon the earth: 26 And though after my skin worms destroy this body, yet in my flesh shall I see God: 27 Whom I shall see for myself, and mine eyes shall behold, and not another; though my reins be consumed within me.

DECLARED BY JESUS

> John 11:25 Jesus said unto her, I am the resurrection, and the life: he that believeth in me, though he were dead, yet shall he live:
> John 14: 19 Yet a little while, and the world seeth me no more; but ye see me: because I live, ye shall live also.
> John 14: 14:1 Let not your heart be troubled: ye believe in God, believe also in me.

2 In my Father's house are many mansions: if it were not so, I would have told you. I go to prepare a place for you.

3 And if I go and prepare a place for you, I will come again, and receive you unto myself; that where I am, there ye may be also.

4 And whither I go ye know, and the way ye know.

5 Thomas saith unto him, Lord, we know not whither thou goest; and how can we know the way?

6 Jesus saith unto him, I am the way, the truth, and the life: no man cometh unto the Father, but by me.

DEVELOPED BY THE BIBLE:

481 times it speaks of heaven.

DESCRIBED BY JOHN

Rev. 4:1 After this I looked, and, behold, a door was opened in heaven: and the first voice which I heard was as it were of a trumpet talking with me; which said, Come up hither, and I will show thee things which must be hereafter.

2 And immediately I was in the spirit; and, behold, a throne was set in heaven, and one sat on the throne.

3 And he that sat was to look upon like a jasper and a sardine stone: and there was a rainbow round about the throne, in sight like unto an emerald.

4 And round about the throne were four and twenty seats: and upon the seats I saw four and twenty elders sitting, clothed in white raiment; and they had on their heads crowns of gold.

Rev. 21:1  And I saw a new heaven and a new earth: for the first heaven and the first earth were passed away; and there was no more sea.

2    And I John saw the holy city, new Jerusalem, coming down from God out of heaven, prepared as a bride adorned for her husband.

3   And I heard a great voice out of heaven saying, Behold, the tabernacle of God is with men, and he will dwell with them, and they shall be his people, and God himself shall be with them, and be their God.

## DELIGHT OF MY SOUL

1 Cor. 15:55 O death, where is thy sting? O grave, where is thy victory?

1 Cor. 15:57 But thanks be to God, which giveth us the victory through our Lord Jesus Christ. 58 Therefore, my beloved brethren, be ye steadfast, unmovable, always abounding in the work of the Lord, forasmuch as ye know that your labour is not in vain in the Lord.

## REAL PLACE:

I Kings 8:30  And hearken thou to the supplication of thy servant, and of thy people Israel, when they shall pray toward this place: <u>and hear thou in heaven thy dwelling place</u>: and when thou hearest, forgive.

Matt.6: 9  After this manner therefore pray ye: Our Father <u>which art in heaven</u>, Hallowed be thy name.

Phil. 3:20 For our (citizenship) conversation <u>is in heaven</u>; from whence also we look for the Saviour, the Lord Jesus Christ: 21 Who shall change our vile body, that it may be fashioned like unto his glorious body, according to the working whereby he is able even to subdue all things unto himself.

2 Cor. 5:1 For we know that if our earthly house of this tabernacle were dissolved, we have a building of God, an house not made with hands, <u>eternal in the heavens.</u>

HEAVEN IS READY:

2 Cor. 5: 8 We are confident, I say, and willing rather to be absent from the body, and to be present with the Lord.
Steven – Paul

HEAVEN IS RIGHT:

A young minister came to me concerning the lottery and wanted to get my opinion about it. "I really could use the money. My bills are eating me up."
I replied, you want me to agree that if you win the 13 million that it would be right? "Yes, I suppose that is what I am wondering."
Well, I said, if you lost then we must consider it would be His way of saying its wrong! "Wow, I hadn't thought of it that way."
I knew the chances were far more that he would lost than winning.

God's promise is that if you give to His church He will restore it a hundred fold.

## HEAVEN IS RESTORATION:

Rev. 21: 4 And God shall wipe away all tears from their eyes; and there shall be no more death, neither sorrow, nor crying, neither shall there be any more pain: for the former things are passed away.

5 And he that sat upon the throne said, Behold, I make all things new. And he said unto me, Write: for these words are true and faithful.

6 And he said unto me, It is done. I am Alpha and Omega, the beginning and the end. I will give unto him that is athirst of the fountain of the water of life freely.

7. He that overcometh shall inherit all things; and I will be his God, and he shall be my son.

---

ILLUSTRATION: 1995 Promise Keepers men meeting in San Diego. Young man went forward to be saved.-"Please pray for my wife!"

---

Rev. 22: 3 And there shall be no more curse: but the throne of God and of the Lamb shall be in it; and his servants shall serve him:

4 And they shall see his face; and his name shall be in their foreheads.

5 And there shall be no night there; and they need no candle, neither light of the sun; for the Lord God giveth them light: and they shall reign for ever and ever.

## HEAVEN IS REWARD:

Rev. 21:24 And the nations of them which are saved shall walk in the light of it: and the kings of the earth do bring their glory and honour into it.

25 And the gates of it shall not be shut at all by day: for there shall be no night there.

26 And they shall bring the glory and honour of the nations into it.

Rev. 22:12 And, behold, I come quickly; and my reward is with me, to give every man according as his work shall be.

ILLUSTRATION: Money will buy a bed but not sleep; books but not brains; food but not appetite; finery but not beauty; a house but not a home; medicine but not health; luxuries but not culture; amusements but not happiness; religion but not salvation—a passport to everywhere but heaven.

## HEAVEN IS REUNION:

Our son, our parents, our friends

ILLUSTRATION: SPECIAL OLYMPICS-100 METERS RACE SEVEN SPECIAL CHILDREN...ONE FELL. ALL STOPPED

## HEAVEN IS RESTRICTED:

Rev. 20: 11 And I saw a great white throne, and him that sat on it, from whose face the earth and the heaven fled away; and there was found no place for them.

12 And I saw the dead, small and great, stand before God; and the books were opened: and another book was opened, which is the book of life: and the dead were judged out of those things which were written in the books, according to their works.

13 And the sea gave up the dead which were in it; and death and hell delivered up the dead which were in them: and they were judged every man according to their works.

Rev. 21:8 But the fearful, and unbelieving, and the abominable, and murderers, and whoremongers, and sorcerers, and idolaters, and all liars, shall have their part in the lake which burneth with fire and brimstone: which is the second death.

Rev. 21: 27 And there shall in no wise enter into it any thing that defileth, neither whatsoever worketh abomination, or maketh a lie: but they which are written in the Lamb's book of life.

Rev. 22: 15 For without are dogs, and sorcerers, and whoremongers, and murderers, and idolaters, and whosoever loveth and maketh a lie.

Conclusion:
John Jasper – Served God in excitement
Arnold Pollard- Believe God in trouble times

Pastor Ki- Sold out to God when no one seemed to care but God.

CHARLEY MC COY...AT AGE 72 was given keys to Florida by his church after he had pastored 56 years in Long Island, NY, but did feel his ministry was over. Died at age 88 in India in an evaluator while going to speak to the YMCA there. He was a chief confident to the Famous Soong Sisters and the first President of the Republic of China. No his ministry was greater after his retirement.

# 12

## BEING AND DOING

Psalm 78:70-72
Rev. David Williford
Institutional Advancement at Welch College
Preach at Canaan Land, Grove City

The 78th Psalm is a treasure trove of preaching and teaching material. It can be especially helpful with young converts because it is a concise history of Israel from their redemption out of Egypt until David is crowned King. For new converts, who often struggle with the chronology of the Old Testament, it can be a good basic primer.

The chapter ends with the ascension of David to the throne, and includes four descriptive phrases that give insight into the greatness of David. He is characterized as a man of humility, compassion, integrity, and excellence. For the sake of time and space I will focus only on the last two phrases, and will build two life principles that flow from them.

Principle one is found in the phrase, "...he fed them according to the integrity of his heart." The word "integrity" means wholeness, fullness, completeness. The writer is saying what God said of David, that he was a man after God's own heart. (Acts 13:22) David's service then flowed out of a heart totally devoted to God. What he was gave rise to what he did, not vice versa.

In this phrase is found a basic principle of the Christian life: *What you are is more important than what you do.* The writer tells us what David did, he fed the people of God, but more important than what he did was that his actions flowed out of a heart of integrity.

That is important because we're often tempted to reverse the order. In the Christian life it is really easy to fall into the temptation to do and not be. We can know all of the lingo, all of the phrases, we know how to act when we're in church or around church people, and we can do all the right things, even though our heart may not be right with God.

You can teach a Sunday School class and be backslidden. You can sing in the choir, or sing a solo in front of the church while you're harboring sin in your heart. You can go on visitation right after you and your wife have had a battle royal at home. You can pray, preach, teach, sing...all the right things, all the good activities, and be totally out of the will of God. It is easy for our actions to be right while our heart is wrong.

But that was never the way God intended it. His plan has always been for our doing to flow out of, or be a result of what we are. Our actions are to flow from and be an expression of our heart. Sadly, we've learned to go through the motions without our heart being what it needs to be.

In the late 19th century D.L. Moody was preaching a crusade in London. He was interviewed by a newspaper reporter who asked the question, "Mr. Moody, what is the greatest sin one can commit?"

If we were to run a survey in our churches, I wonder what the response would be. Some would probably say adultery, because the marriage relationship symbolizes our relationship to Christ, and to be unfaithful to Him is the highest betrayal. Others might say murder, because it involves the taking of a life created in the image of God, and no amount of repentance or sorrow can undo that action.

Interestingly, Moody did not reference any of the sins we might think. In fact, he did not name a specific sin, but responded instead with a question of his own: "What is the greatest commandment?" he asked the reporter. "That's simple sir," the reporter responded. "Jesus said, 'Thou shalt love the Lord thy God with all thy heart, and with all thy soul, and with all thy mind. This is the first and great commandment.'" (Matthew 22:37-38). Moody replied, "Doesn't it make sense that the greatest sin would be the transgression of the greatest commandment?"

I'm not sure about you, but that makes me more than a little uncomfortable. When I see the problems facing our world and our country I want to look outside the church and point fingers at the secularists, the pornographers, the drug dealers, the militant homosexual activists, and say, "There's our problem, that's what killing our country and weakening our churches."

But the reality is, the thing that is killing churches and our nation is not outside the church, but inside the church. In the words of the comic strip character Pogo, "We have met the enemy and he is us." It is not the world that is hindering the church, it is we who are redeemed, part of the family of God, who have ceased to be and have relied on what we do, going through the motions with no true spiritual impetus behind our actions. That, my friends, is what is sapping the life, strength, and vitality out of the Church! And the truth is, most of us are guilty, to one degree or another.

Jesus wrote, through John, seven letters to churches in Asia Minor while John was on Patmos. The first, to the church at Ephesus, was glowing with commendation for the church. He praised their service and their ministry, their doctrinal purity, and their refusal to compromise truth. But at the end of the letter He gives one indictment: "...I have somewhat against thee because thou hast left thy first love." (Revelation 2:4)

This was a church that had an impressive spiritual pedigree. It was founded by Paul and later pastored by Timothy. Our past heritage is not a guarantee that we will never fall into the trap of a lackadaisical relationship with our Lord. We must, at all times, guard the affection and fervor of our heart lest we fall into the trap of doing without being.

A half-hearted love will eventually lead us into a lukewarm state. The church at Laodicea had fallen into a place of lukewarm devotion, and it greatly concerned Jesus. He had not one word of commendation for that congregation, even telling them that he would prefer they be cold rather than lukewarm.

I submit to you that it is a short move, both geographically and spiritually, to move from Ephesus to Laodicea. If our heart issues are not guarded in Ephesus, we will find ourselves living in Laodicea.

The first part of verse 72 gave us our first principle, and the latter part of that verse gives us our second. He guided Israel, "...by the skillfulness of his hands." What David did, he did for the right reason, because of his love for God. Because he loved God, what he did, he did with excellence.

Said another way, what David did, he did well. His efforts were not half-hearted or just enough to do the job. It was masterfully done. David was not content to do the job just well enough to fulfill the requirements of what he was charged to do. He wanted to serve with excellence. That is our second life principle: What you do, do to the best of your ability.

The wise man said, "Whatsoever thy hand findeth to do, do it with thy might." (Ecclesiastes 9:10) This goes so contrary to the attitude with which most today approach life, work, and even ministry. The prevailing spirit today seems to be, "Do just enough to get by, just enough to satisfy my employer, and just enough that will allow me to say that the job is done."

May I submit to you that that mindset is found even in the church, and it is destroying us. Where is our appreciation for excellence? Our determination to do the very best that we can? We need to remember that our service is "unto the Lord" and that He is not satisfied with the slipshod, the second best. Malachi severely chastised the people of his day because the gifts they brought for sacrifice were inferior, and thus unworthy of being offered to the LORD.

When we think of what we do for the Lord, is it our intention to give Him our very best, or are we just giving Him the leftovers, the half-hearted, and the mediocre?

A number of years ago I read a book by Frank Tillapaugh, *The Church Unleashed.* In it he discussed the concept he called, "Concerned Neglect." Basically, if no one felt led to undertake a particular ministry the church did not try to do it. It wasn't that they were uncaring. Areas of ministry that went undone were the focus of special prayer, asking God to raise up someone who would feel the burden and undertake the ministry.

I incorporated that somewhat into the church where I served. If no one wanted to teach the junior class, we split the students, putting the older students with the class above them and the younger with the class below. When folks protested my answer was, "These kids deserve to have a teacher who feels that their teaching job is a ministry for God, and they are going to give it 100%

effort. These kids are too valuable to place with a teacher who is only teaching the class because no one else will do it."

There were years we restructured classes, did not have certain events, because we felt it was too important to do poorly. We feared that someone who was just filling the space because no one else would do it would not give themselves wholly to it. We wanted to avoid the mediocre and strive for excellence, because service to the Lord demands that.

How does this play out in practical terms? If you teach a class, make sure you're prepared. Put in the study time necessary to teach well. If you sing, practice. Don't just "wing it" because you happen to be talented. Put in the time to make sure that when you offer that song as an act of worship to God, that it will be done to the very best of your ability. Our God deserves no less.

But the reality is that this principle should apply to more than just what we do at church. It should actually govern how we live our lives. One of the downfalls of our thinking is the way we separate, in our minds, the activity of full time Christian workers from laity, men and women who are not involved in full time vocational ministry.

We think of preachers, missionaries, etc., as being "called by God" (and they are), but when it comes to laity, we seem to think that their work or career is somehow different. We think preachers should earnestly seek God's will about ministry positions and potential moves (and they should), but we don't think laymen and women have the same responsibility.

You remember that in Ephesians 2:8-10 Paul gives that marvelous declaration that salvation is by faith, through grace, and not by works. But remember that in verse 10 he reminds us that we, all of God's redeemed, are "...His workmanship, created in Christ Jesus unto good works, which God hath before ordained that we should walk in them."

Said another way, God has a will for the life of each of His children, and we should find that will and serve Him effectively in it. God does not call every believer to full-time vocational church ministry positions like being a pastor, missionary, or the like, but He does have a plan for every believer.

God wants some believers in the field of medicine, some in education, some in the mental health field. He wants some in business, some in the factory, and some in the skilled trades. Find the area where God has gifted you, or given you a skill set, and in your 8-5 job each day, determine that you are going to glorify God through it. See your vocation as your place of ministry, and determine that every day you will glorify God by doing your job to the very best of your ability. Your primary motive at work should not be to keep the boss happy or to try and advance within the system. Your primary motive should be to offer your labor, each day, as an act of worship to God so He will be pleased with your efforts.

That attitude will revolutionize how you approach work. No longer is it the drudgery you have to endure to make it to the weekend, but it is now seen as an act of spiritual worship each day. And when that becomes your attitude, and you perform each day to the best of your ability, you'll be amazed at what God will do and how He will use you. You may find that your greatest contribution to God's kingdom will take place there, even more than the things you do in your local church.

Let me give you one example of how this can take place. A number of years ago a young man was in college preparing to go to China as a missionary. While he was in school he competed in track events. He was a really good athlete, and excelled in both track and rugby competition.

His sister chided him on one occasion about his involvement in athletics, suggesting that he was wasting his time. After a lot of thought and counsel he eventually told her that he felt God had given him the ability to run well, and by doing that he could honor God. He told her, "God made me fast, and when I run I feel His pleasure."

He was good enough that he was selected to join his country's track team and represent the nation at the Olympic Games that were to be held in Paris. He was scheduled to run the 100 meter race, but when he arrived in Paris he discovered that the preliminary race, one he had to run in order to qualify for the finals, was scheduled on a Sunday.

He was a Scottish Presbyterian and held a very high view of what one did and did not do on Sunday, so he told his coach he could not participate in a race on Sunday. He would be in church, and would use that day to worship, pray, and mediate.

He was put under enormous pressure to change his mind. Teammates tried to change his mind, newspaper editorials were written criticizing his decision, and eventually a member of the royal family even visited with him, trying to change his mind.

However, he stayed firm in his decision.

Finally the decision was made that he would compete in another event that did not require him to run on Sunday. He was placed in the 400 meter competition, even though most folks gave him little chance to have any success.

The reason most folks gave him so little chance of success is that the two races, 100 meter and 400 meter, are two totally different type races. Generally two different type athletes run those races, and the training regime is completely different. And remember that he is running against the very best in the world in the Olympics. But to the amazement of almost everyone, he qualified for the finals of the event.

As he was preparing to run in the finals that would determine who would win the Olympic medal, a runner from America walked up to him and without saying a word, shook his hand and handed him a note. The note was an Old Testament quote and simply said, "...them that honor me, I will honor." (I Samuel 2:30.)

He took that piece of paper, grasped it in his hand, and ran the race. To the amazement of almost everyone watching, he not only won the race, but he set a new world record in that 1924 Olympic Games. He won a most unlikely victory, and honored God as he did.

You say, "Wow. That's almost a story book ending. Someone should make a movie about it." Someone did. In 1981 *Chariots of Fire* took the movie world by storm and won an Oscar for telling the story of the Scottish runner Eric Liddell and his devotion to God. It is a story of faith and faithfulness that illustrates what complete devotion looks like.

But may I play Paul Harvey and tell you "the rest of the story"? Remember that I told you that Liddell was preparing to go to China as a missionary? He eventually went to China, serving from 1925 to 1943. In 1943, as a result of the Japanese invasion of China, Liddell was placed in a prisoner of war camp. While there he did the same things he had done before being arrested: he taught Bible clubs for kids, served the elderly, and developed relationships with people so he could share Christ with them.

He died from an inoperable brain tumor in 1945 while still a prisoner.

The amazing thing is, most people don't know the story of Eric Liddell the missionary. They know the story of

Eric Liddell the Olympic gold medalist who was so devoted to Christ that he refused to run on Sunday. *Chariots of Fire* ends with the Olympic Games, it doesn't tell the story of Eric the missionary.

What I'm trying to convey to you is that God can take what you do you in sports, in music, in the workplace, in the factory, in the classroom, and use it to impact the lives of people. Don't live your life in a half-hearted or slipshod manner because you think what you do and how you do it doesn't matter, because it does!

Live your life as an act of service and worship to God, do it with excellence, and God will honor that effort. I beg of you, seek excellence in all you do.

So, these are the two principles: (1) What you are is more important than what you do, (2) What you do, do it with excellence. Those two principles, adopted and lived out, will change your life...it will change your church...it can change our world.

I beg you, guard your heart and your love for Christ. Be passionately in love with Him. And serve Him with excellence, not only through the things we traditionally think of as Christian ministry, but in everyday life. Then sit back and be amazed at what God will do through you.

# MINISTERIAL PLEDGE

*Be It Hereby Resolved*
*That I serve a God who never changes. He never has and never will. His nature is not dependent on my understanding. My view of Him will not be determined by my circumstances.*

*Be It Hereby Resolved*
*That God died a horrible death to save me from eternal damnation. He chose to save me because I was incompetent and hopeless. For some inexplicable reason, I appealed to Him in this state, and His love for me is a gift.*

*Be It Hereby Resolved*
*That I will never forget my capacity to sin, and I will always be amazed at God's capacity for Grace.*

*Be It Hereby Resolved*
*That I am a powerful person because the King of Kings delights to make me strong. Living by Faith, I choose to live in the power of each moment rather than regret my past or fear my future. My life may be exciting and satisfying, but not necessarily comfortable or safe.*

*Be It Hereby Resolved*

*That my life will demonstrate Love and Grace more than any other virtues. I may consider, but I will not be stifled by rules, religion, denomination or conservatism.*

*Be It Hereby Resolved*
*That my home is where He is. By His design, I live here, and He lives in me. However, soon, my residence will be in a different dimension. I accept these truths even though they are a mystery to me.*

*Be It Hereby Resolved*
*That my life will continue after I die on this Earth. Death holds no power over me or the ones I love. I will never stop longing for that place which I have never seen.*